EDINBURGH UNIVERSITY PUBLICATIONS

LANGUAGE & LITERATURE No. 2

THE EDINBURGH UNIVERSITY PRESS
Sole Agent
OLIVER AND BOYD
TWEEDDALE COURT, EDINBURGH
98 GREAT RUSSELL STREET
LONDON W.C.

ANGLO-NORMAN IN THE CLOISTERS

THE INFLUENCE OF
THE ORDERS
UPON ANGLO-NORMAN
LITERATURE

BY

M. DOMINICA LEGGE

EDINBURGH
AT THE UNIVERSITY PRESS
1950

PRINTED IN GREAT BRITAIN
BY R. AND R. CLARK, LTD., EDINBURGH

PREFACE

THIS is a short book, but it has been long in preparation. The subject was first publicly broached in a course of lectures delivered at Oxford in the Michaelmas Term of 1938, and dealt with more fully in a paper read before the Mediaeval Society in Oxford in 1943. Its conception, however, goes back to my first researches in Anglo-Norman, and I am grateful to many for inspiration, perhaps chiefly to the late Professor Paul Studer, who first suggested to me the *Life of St. Modwenna*, St. Edmund's *Merure* and Peter of Peckham's *Lumere as Lais* as subjects of research, Dr. Hastings Rashdall and Dr. G. G. Coulton. The fact that I have been able to inspect nearly every manuscript mentioned on this side of the Atlantic is mainly due to my tenure of the Mary Somerville Research Fellowship at Somerville College.

The book is heavily weighted with footnotes, but in order to keep them within bounds, reference by means of figures in square brackets has been made to the bibliography in J. Vising's *Anglo-Norman Language and Literature* (London, 1923), and as a rule only the most recent edition of a text is mentioned. Wherever possible I have referred to forthcoming works, but it is characteristic of this kind of survey that it is out of date before it is published. I am acutely aware, too, of the fact that there must be many gaps which readers will fill in for themselves, but I hope with feelings of indulgence, for if writers of studies of this kind stopped to count the cost they would never have the courage to begin, much less finish, and yet, however incomplete, general surveys have their uses.

I wish, in concluding, to express my best thanks to Professor M. K. Pope, Professor John Orr and my Mother for reading the

v

235811

book in typescript, and to Sir F. M. Powicke for offering advice from which I have endeavoured to profit. Professor Orr has placed me still further in his debt by his kind assistance in correcting proofs. I am proud that publication should have been undertaken by the Edinburgh University Press.

M. Dominica Legge

Edinburgh, 1948

CONTENTS

I

INTRODUCTION

WHEN the passer-by pushes open the south door of the Church of the Holy Rood in the remote village of Wood Eaton, his eye lights upon the figure of the giant Christopher on the wall opposite, bearing the comforting legend :

> Ki cest image verra
> Le ivr de male mort ne mvrra.

(He who shall look upon this picture that day shall not make a bad death.)

These words are a reminder of the time when all England was bilingual, and much of it was trilingual, when a monk could write :

> Translaté l'ai desqu'a la fin
> E de l'engleis e del latin
> Q'en franceis le poent entendre
> Li grant, [li mien] e li mendre.[1]

(I have translated it to the end both from the English and from the Latin, for the great, [the middling] and the least are all able to understand it in French.)

It has recently become the fashion to fight the Battle of Hastings o'er again, and to revive the fallacies upon which a novelist, for perfectly legitimate reasons, based his romance of Ivanhoe. This fashion is displeasing, as any distortion of the truth is bound to be, and it smacks at once of the racialism which is one of the causes of our present discontents and of the class-

---

[1] Denis Pyramus, quoted by J. Vising, *Anglo-Norman Language and Literature* (London, 1923), p. 15.

warfare which is another. Fortunately, we have witnesses to the true state of affairs. Bishop Fitz Nigel described the fusion of the Norman and Anglo-Saxon peoples in the *Dialogus de Scaccario* in happy ignorance of the theories of Adolf Hitler or Karl Marx. The English people have been one since the Battle of the Standard, and the descendants of those who fought the Battle of Harlaw can only envy them their good fortune and wonder at their folly in reviving controversies long since dead.

Prejudice apart, however, Anglo-Norman suffers from being neither flesh nor fish, nor good red herring. To the Frenchman, it seems a barbaric off-shoot of his own language and literature : to the Englishman, it is a troublesome foreign tongue today. Both should have more patience. Some, even if it is only a little, of the best of Old French literature was written in England, and the French are everlastingly in England's debt for the way in which their most remarkable texts, including what they now regard as their national epic, were transcribed and preserved on English soil. The traditions often regarded as peculiar to Middle English literature had already been developed in Anglo-Norman, and translators and adaptors are given the credit which rightly belongs to their predecessors. Both French and English lose by neglecting this link which in the past was forged between them.

Anglo-Norman literature has a serious and didactic bias, which has never been satisfactorily explained, unless that it was written by and for a decent, law-abiding people. It has sometimes been suggested that the reason for this bias is that Anglo-Norman was only written by clerks, but to this it may be objected that since in the Middle Ages only clerks were literate, the same condition applies to most mediaeval literature (save the lyric and some romance), and would seem to imply that there was in England a lower proportion of " stickit " clerks than elsewhere. It may be that " cloisterers ", to use Chaucer's word, did produce more vernacular literature, and of a different kind, in England than in France, and this seems a reason for finding out exactly what they did write.

Most mediaeval literature is anonymous, and even if the name of a writer is preserved, that is very often the sum of what is known about him. John Doe, Friar Minor, seems to have a little more personality than plain Richard Roe. The study of the writings of men of religion is a means of breaching a wall of mystery which is apt to surround a mediaeval author, yet too much must not be expected. The men of the Middle Ages were individualists, and the study of the individual must remain at least as important as the study of the Order to which he belonged.

The two main questions which fall to be answered are, whether the fact of belonging to an Order had any influence on the type of work produced by an individual, and whether the Orders as such made a definite contribution to literature. The results which follow from this investigation will be found to be meagre, but they are none the less interesting and should clear the ground for future work on Anglo-Norman literature.

The late Joseph Bédier, it will be remembered, had visions of monks along the Pilgrim Routes of France holding " Press conferences " at which professional *jongleurs* received " hand-outs ". The *chansons de geste* of the great cycles did not originate in England, but something of the same sort might have taken place on a smaller scale. That this is unlikely will presently appear. Monks and nuns seem to have been capable of doing their own vulgarisation. There is little difference in method between the clerk and the *jongleur*, and often not much in subject. This is apparent in M. Faral's book on the *Jongleurs*, and more evidence of it will be produced in due course.

In considering the writings produced by members of Religious Orders in England, pride of place must naturally be given to the oldest and greatest of the Western Orders—the Benedictines. St. Benedict had no intention of creating an Order of scholars and teachers. His monks were to be dedicated to the service of God and all other work was to be secondary to that. Yet the conditions of Benedictine life are peculiarly favourable to men of a scholarly turn of mind, and thus it is that so many scholars have been Benedictines, while it would be untrue to say that they were scholars because they were Benedictines. These scholars have sometimes appeared singly, like Bede, and sometimes in such battalions that they have required a separate organisation, like the Maurists. The Benedictines were not founded to write, any more than their daughter Order, the Cistercians, were founded to farm sheep, and yet the Benedictines took to writing as inevitably as the Cistercians did to sheep-farming.

Not all the famous Benedictine Houses of mediaeval England are represented, and indeed two of them, St. Albans and Bury St. Edmunds—two of the " pedigree " monasteries, as Professor Galbraith calls them—outclass all the rest. There is no evidence here that the monasteries of the Welsh March helped in the spread of Celtic stories. The answer to that problem more likely belongs to the province of Latin literature.

After the Benedictines, the Cistercians are poorly represented. They seem to have written little in England compared with France, but they were accused of an interest in secular literature.[1] The catalogue of books belonging to a Cistercian House bears this out, and the one monk to be mentioned later who wrote for his fellows and not for outsiders was probably a Cistercian.

Other Orders of monks are hardly represented at all, though there is one Templar on the list. The Austin Canons rank next to the Benedictines in number and importance, and the only women writers seem to have been among the Benedictines and the Canonesses. Of the two original Orders of Friars, the Franciscans were much more important than the Dominicans as writers in Anglo-Norman.

The survey will be completed by brief mention of works written by secular clergy for purposes of comparison, and by the study of two side-issues, the spread of the knowledge of literature by means of the monastic library and the strolling minstrel, and the influence of patrons upon literature.

[1] Cf. D. Knowles, *The Monastic Order in England* (Cambridge, 1940), p. 260.

There is little material here, either historical or literary, that is new, and opinions are bound to differ upon questions of interpretation. But this is the first attempt to treat the subject as a whole. It is a chapter in the history of Anglo-Norman literature, a history which has yet to be written. The late Johann Vising's bibliography of printed and manuscript sources, *Anglo-Norman Language and Literature* (London, 1923), remains an indispensable starting-point for all research in Anglo-Norman, but it is over twenty years old and is in need of revision. The late E. Walberg's lectures to the École des Chartes deal with his own particular province and are deliberately entitled *Quelques Aspects de la littérature anglo-normande* (Paris, 1936). Here is another " aspect ". The pioneer work in the field covered here was done by the Abbé de la Rue and Thomas Wright. The texts which they edited no longer satisfy modern requirements, and some of their conclusions have inevitably been falsified in the course of time. Paul Meyer's investigations of manuscripts traced out many a path for others to follow. Works emanating from monasteries and chronicles were made available in the Rolls Series, but the actual texts printed were notorious from the first, and one by one they are having to be re-edited. Much has been done since Paul Studer gave his Inaugural Lecture at Oxford,[1] but the numerous references in the pages which follow to works which have never been published or have only been printed in an unsatisfactory form will show how much still remains to be done.

This investigation, then, is upon lines which do not seem to have been followed before. It is to be hoped that the reason is not that they were not worth following, and that it will blaze the trail for similar studies of literature in other languages.

[1] *The Study of Anglo-Norman* (Oxford, 1920).

II

MONKS OF BURY

OF all the English Benedictine Houses, Bury St. Edmunds was one of the greatest, and it happens also to be the best-documented of monasteries. It has, from first to last, been favoured by fortune, and it is not surprising to find that it was prolific in writers, and that the names of these writers should have survived. The list of works written at Bury starts, appropriately enough, with a twelfth-century *Life* of the patron saint of the Abbey.[1] Denis Pyramus, the author, had been, according to his own account, a court poet in his youth, a writer of lyrics and love-songs after the Provençal model. He may even have been, like Frère Angier, of Continental birth, though this is unlikely. It is thought that he must have been under the patronage of Henry II or of his Queen, and he was probably an associate and rival of Marie de France and the anonymous author of the *Partenopeus of Blois*, whom he condemns as writers of stories and lies. But now :

> Mes jurs jolifs de ma joefnesce
> S'en vunt ; si trey jeo a veilesce.
> Si est bien dreit ke me repente :
> En autre oure metterai m'entente. (ll. 17 ss.)

(My gay days of my youth are passing, and I approach old age. So it is fitting that I should repent : I shall turn my mind to other things.) He had probably retired to the Abbey of St. Edmunds-

---

[1] [14.] Latest and best edition : H. Kjellman (Göteborg, 1935). The quotations are from the more accessible edition of T. Arnold in *Memorials of St. Edmund's Abbey* (Rolls Series, xciv).

bury. It is not only in the pages of romance that a man would end his days in a state of " moniage ".[1]

No mention is made in this poem of any particular patron. It is meant to be read aloud, as entertainment, and the audience, like the audience of any romance or *chanson de geste*, is addressed as " segnur ", and qualified once as " cristiene gent " (l. 95). The work falls into the conventional two parts, the first being the *Life* proper, the second the account of the miracles performed by the saint's remains. The second part opens thus :

> Translaté avum l'aventure
> Solum le livre e le scripture,
> De Seint Edmund, coment il vint
> En Engletere, que il tint,
> Dunt rey fu tant cum il vesquit,
> E del martir qu'il suffrit.
> Translaté l'ai desque a la fin,
> E del Engleis e del Latin,
> Que en Franceis le poent entendre
> E li grant e li mendre.   (ll. 3259 ss.)

(We have translated what happened according to the book and the writing, about St. Edmund, how he came to England, which he held, of which he was King as long as he lived, and about the marytrdom which he suffered. I have translated it to the end, both from the English and from the Latin, for both the great and the least can understand it in French.)   The Latin sources have been identified by Arnold and by Henry H. Haxo,[2] but the English sources have yet to be traced with the same degree of certainty.

It is unlikely that a man of Denis Pyramus's attainments would be allowed to live the life of a hermit if he chose to retire from the world to a community as busy and as important as that of St. Edmund's, and this is a reason, as well as the probable coincidence of dates, for accepting Haxo's tentative identification of Denis with Magister Dionysius the Cellarer, the rival of

---

[1] Cf. L. Petit de Julleville, *Histoire de la langue et de la littérature française* (Paris, 1896), ii. 163.   [2] *Modern Philology*, xii (1914-15), pp. 345-66, 559-83.

Samson and ultimately the mouthpiece of the convent in securing the election of that most famous of Abbots. This Dionysius was first mentioned in 1173 and was dead by 1214. He had been banished in the troublous reign of the feeble Hugo, and therefore probably wrote in the time of the enthusiastic Samson, who in his early days had himself re-written the history of the *Miracles* of St. Edmund in Latin. Yet the first few years of Abbot Samson were hardly restful, and it is difficult to see what leisure or occasion a writer would have had for composition in the seventies and eighties, unless the poem was intended to entertain the laity at the " Great Gaudy " at the installation of Samson in 1182. The manuscript, unfortunately, is incomplete, and there is no means of knowing whether there was once an epilogue with further biographical details, or how recent were the last miracles recorded in the poem. The latest editor dates the text, mainly on linguistic grounds, between 1170 and 1180 ; Professor Pope, on the same grounds, would prefer to date it nearer the end of the century.[1]

One of Denis's sources, the *Infancy* by Gaufridus De Fontibus, was written in the time of Abbot Ording, 1148–56. 1156 is therefore an absolute point of departure for the dating but it is too early to be of any real help. The text also provides some internal evidence of date by its references to Marie de France's *Lais* and the *Partenopeus of Blois*, but unfortunately neither of these can be dated and Denis Pyramus is used as evidence for dating the *Lais* themselves. Marie de France, however, is of some help. Denis only mentions her *Lais*, the earliest of her works, which was followed by the *Fables*, and finally by *St. Patrick's Purgatory*, which was probably written after 1189.[2] It is therefore possible, though of course quite uncertain, that Denis was writing before she too turned pious and wrote the *Purgatory*. In any case, the *Lais* were most likely written nearer 1180 than 1170, and on every ground a date in the eighties or

---

[1] Kjellman, pp. cxxii ss. Cf. Review by M. K. Pope, *Modern Language Review*, xxxi (1936), pp. 575-6.   [2] Cf. A. Ewert, *Marie de France, Lais* (Oxford, 1944), pp. vi-x.

> N'ai or ne argent en ma baillie.
> Pri Deu k'après ceste vie
> En regne celestien
> Regner pusse of vus. Amen.

(Let me offer you this work, my poverty has no wider scope. I have neither gold nor silver in my possession. I pray God that after this life I may reign with you in the heavenly kingdom.)

The other contains the earliest apology for imperfections of language which Vising was able to discover :

> Ore pri chescun ki lit e ot
> Cest treité, s'en aucun mot
> Mesprein, k'il l'amender voile ;
> Kar n'est hom ki ne sumoile.
> Language par pais varie ;
> Si language de France die,
> N'en doi estre a droit repris
> De gent de veisin pais. (ll. 89 ss.)

(Now I pray each one who reads and hears this treatise, that if I am wrong in any word, that he will amend it. For there is no man who does not nod. Language varies according to district ; if I speak the language of France, I ought not by rights to be reproved by people of a neighbouring country.) Exactly how this apology is to be interpreted is a little obscure. In any case, too much ought not to be made of these remarks, which were far from being peculiar to Anglo-Norman as Vising seems to imply. They are to be found in most texts with a strong dialectal flavour, and Pontoise, with its almost Parisian accent, seems to have been a kind of Wigan in its day.[1] In this particular case, the apology for language follows directly after the conventional apology for imperfections of sense or matter, which, as will have been seen, was commonly put in epilogues, partly from mock-humility, partly to cover the author in case any heresy-hunt was instituted against him.

Thirdly, much about the same time as the *Life* of Edward the

---

[1] Cf. Petit de Julleville, *op. cit.* ii. 461.

C

Confessor, the *Life* of Thomas à Becket [101], the second therefore to be written in this monastery. This version exists today
only in fragments, and was edited, with facsimiles, by Paul Meyer
for the Société des anciens textes français in 1885. Paul Meyer
considered the question of Matthew Paris's authorship, but re-
jected it on the grounds that the MS. is not written in the same
hand as that of *St. Alban*. The matter has been reopened by
Dr. James and the claim of Matthew Paris vindicated. The poem
is in the same style as the *Life* of Edward the Confessor, with
the same high proportion of seven syllable lines mixed with the
octosyllables which is characteristic not only of that *Life* but of
the *St. Alban* rubrics. The disposition of the *Lives* of St.
Thomas and St. Edward is compared by Paul Meyer (p. xxxix).
The layout of the two MSS. and their ornamentation are similar,
though the *Life* of St. Thomas has headings in Latin and one folio
has only two columns of writing instead of three. Its leaves are
about 2 mm. higher than those of the *St. Edward* MS., though
those of the latter may, of course, have been cut down. It is
therefore possible that the two were originally part of the same
volume, and the fact that more than one hand seems to have been
at work is no obstacle to this proposition. It is, however, more
likely that the two MSS. represent different " editions ", and the
fact that the two *Lives* were originally bound together in a copy
which cannot have been presented to the Queen, as it is supposed
was done in the case of the *St. Edward* MS., is proved by the note
on a fly-leaf of the *St. Alban* MS., a note which Dr. James dated
about 1250, and translated as follows : " G. Send, please, to the
lady countess of Arundel, Isabel, that she is to send you the book
about St. Thomas the Martyr and St. Edward which I translated
and portrayed and which the lady countess of Cornwall may keep
until Whitsuntide."

A note ascribed to Thomas of Walsingham records [1] that
Matthew Paris had written and illustrated the *Lives* of Sts.
Amphibalus and Alban, and also of Sts. Thomas and Edmund,

---

[1] *Amundesham's Annals* (R.S. xxviii), ii. 303.

Archbishops of Canterbury. Of these there are therefore still in existence the illustrated *Lives* of the two martyrs, in entirety, and of St. Thomas, in fragments. The *Life* of St. Edward is not mentioned by Walsingham, but he cannot have written Edmund in mistake for Edward, for he is referring to an Archbishop of Canterbury. Dr. James therefore feared that the *Life* of St. Edmund was lost for ever, though he believed that Cotton MS. Vitellius D VIII had formerly contained a copy of it. It was left to the late Professor Baker to have the joy of discovering the text, unfortunately without its illustrations, in the well-known Welbeck MS. of saints' *Lives*.[1] The rubrics, too, if they ever existed, are missing with the pictures. In this case, Matthew Paris was translating his own work, and Professor Baker was able to identify this in Cotton MS. Julius D VI. The translation is dedicated to Isabelle, Countess of Arundel, wife of Hugh of Albini, the patroness of Wymondham, a cell of St. Albans (ll. 30, 1981). This, therefore, is probably the same lady who had borrowed the *Lives* of Sts. Thomas and Edward, and it may be that she had been inspired by the loan to order a similar *Life* of the other Archbishop connected with Pontigny. Baker put the composition of *St. Edmund* late, after 1247, perhaps even after 1255, which would make it one of Matthew Paris's last works. The traditional date of his death is 1259. Sir F. M. Powicke has questioned this date, which he thinks may be too early (" The Compilation of the ' Chronica Majora ' of Matthew Paris ", *Proceedings of the British Academy*, xxix, communicated July 1944), but Professor V. H. Galbraith argues for the tradition, which in any case cannot be very far wrong (" Roger Wendover and Matthew Paris ", *Glasgow University Publications*, lxi (1944), pp. 29-31).

This is the only work of the kind in which the author names himself. In l. 1692 he refers to himself as " ge Maheu ". It is true that his name may also have appeared on the missing initial folio of the *Life* of St. Alban, but it is to be noted that in the

[1] *Romania*, lv (1929), pp. 332 ss.

St. Edmund he does not mention his name in the prologue, only in the body of the work. Points of detail which recall the *Lives* of St. Thomas or St. Edward are the subject of comments in Professor Baker's footnotes. As usual in Matthew Paris's octo-syllabic verse, short lines are frequent, but perhaps less so than in what may be regarded as the earlier *Lives*, and the editor was able to correct many of them without much difficulty. In this case, the MS. cannot even have been seen by the author, whereas he probably supervised the production of the others, even if he had no hand in it. Hence it is legitimate to emend with a little more freedom. Hiatus is common in this text, as in the others.

This concludes the list of all that appears to survive of Matthew Paris's Anglo-Norman work, but he proposed to write yet another picture book, a project which may have got no further than the plan which fortunately survives on a *St. Alban* fly-leaf. The book was for a Countess of Winchester, presumably either Matilda or Alianor, the second and third wives of Roger de Quincy. Dr. James thought that Matilda, who died in 1252, is the more likely of the two.[1]   The book was to be illustrated by pictures of saints, arranged in pairs, accompanied by explanatory verses in French. The draft for some of these survives. Dr. James conjectured that the book was either a Psalter or a book of Hours. The latter is perhaps more likely to have been illus-trated by pictures of saints. The verses are interesting, for they are quite different from the octosyllable couplets which might have been expected. They are a kind of tail-rhyme. Each saint is allotted half of a six-line stanza. The first two lines are intended to have four syllables each, and rhyme together, while the tail line is of six syllables. Thus the usual arrangement is reversed, and the tail line is longer than the couplet lines.

This book, then, was different in plan and arrangement from the French saints' *Lives*, but it does recall the sequel to the *Lives* of St. Alban and St. Amphibalus. This is an account of the

---

[1] *St. Ædward*, p. 25.

visit of Sts. Germanus and Lupus to Britain, and of King Offa's
foundation of the Abbey.   This is all in Latin, except that the
pictures are accompanied by French rubrics, in this case in the
usual couplets.   Oddly enough, the Latin rubrics of *St. Alban*
are not continued beyond the French text.   In fact, the whole
manuscript is a kind of bilingual production, and this is not surprising since it seems to have been intended for the Abbey itself.
The Countess of Winchester's book, whatever it was, would
most probably be in Latin.   If, as has been suggested, it was a
service-book, the point of the French stanzas would be that they
were easy to remember.   While the psalms were being chanted in
an incomprehensible tongue, the Countess would be able to look
at the pictures, and these would remind her of the verses, which
she could then mutter to herself, for there could be no question
here of following something read aloud.   Once again the laity of
yesterday must be compared to the children of today, who are
often allowed to entertain themselves with Bible pictures during
the delivery of a sermon above their heads.   The reciting of these
verses would be a more profitable exercise than dozing or thinking
about the afternoon's hawking.

The use of pictures, in books or on church walls, was of
course a frequent means of instructing the illiterate in the Middle
Ages, and the vernacular was naturally employed for the benefit of
those who had no Latin.   But it is doubtful whether any other
man combined the two methods as deliberately and as success-
fully as Matthew Paris.   The study of what he did, or caused to
be done, in this way enhances his reputation and makes him an
even more interesting person than the " chiel amang ye takin'
notes ", pictorially or in writing, which is the usual conception of
the great chronicler and administrator.

Incidentally the study of Matthew Paris's French works
should dispose for ever of a curious legend.   This seems to go
back only to 1766, when Bulstrode Whitelocke published his
*Notes upon the King's Writ for choosing Members of Parlia-
ment.*   In this he stated (i. 178) that Matthew Paris wrote that

he was in danger of losing his livelihood because he did not understand the French language. How a monk could lose his livelihood is not divulged. It hardly seems an unfrocking matter. However, this statement was solemnly repeated, although Whitelocke's untrustworthiness is notorious, by A. Luders in his *Essay on the Use of French in our Ancient Laws* (1807, p. 62).[1] It was treated with the contempt it deserved by Sir F. Madden when he edited the *Historia Minor*, in 1869, but this did not stop Sir T. Twist reviving it four years later without a qualm, when he edited the Black Book of the Admiralty (i. liv), also for the Rolls Series. Apparently he had not read his fellow-editor's introduction. So easy it is to scotch, so hard to kill, a mischievous misstatement of this kind.[2]

There remains, however, a difference in quality between the Latin and the French works of Matthew Paris. The limitations forced upon his spirit by his environment have been described by Professor Galbraith,[3] but there is this to add. When Matthew Paris wrote in Latin, he was not deliberately careless. His Anglo-Norman works are his *Opera Minora*, and he does not seem to have taken them so seriously. The same is true of other writers, Grosseteste, for instance, and less famous men like Peter of Peckham. Some, like the author of *St. Brendan*, like Denis Pyramus and Guillaume de Berneville, write well because they cannot help it. St. Edmund's *Merure* was claimed by Professor Robbins as an experiment in metrical prose, and though this is a matter of dispute, the mere fact that the claim could be made is significant. It is a work of great beauty. Thomas of Hales, another mystic, writes with something of the same quality. Absence of style was sometimes deliberately cultivated, a point which will be discussed in a later chapter. In the case of Matthew Paris, the difference between his Latin and his Anglo-Norman writing is partly to be explained as the difference between the way a man

---

[1] *Historia Anglorum* (R.S. xliv), iii. ix.

[2] Whitelocke was probably thinking of Matthew Paris's account of St. Wulstan (*Chronica Majora* (R.S. lvii), ii. 40), cf. Luders, *op. cit.* p. 41. Luders repeated Whitelocke's story without verifying the reference.   [3] *Loc. cit.* pp. 12-13.

writes for publication and the way he writes his letters. Anglo-Norman works were written with an eye to circulation, but the analogy is near enough. Latin was taught, Anglo-Norman was absorbed. There was no standard, and no desire for one.

Beneit and Matthew Paris are the only two writers known to have come from St. Albans itself, but it is probable that another poem is due to an inmate of a cell of that House. This is the text usually known as the *Sermon en Vers* [22]. A better title would be that accorded to it in MS. Digby 86, *Le Romanz de Temtacioun de Secle*. The author, Guischard de Beaulieu, has been the victim of much misrepresentation. Thomas Wright[1] confused him with the Continental Guischard de Beaujeu, who turned Cluniac in his old age. So strong a hold did this idea obtain, that even the late Dr. M. R. James was once guilty of emending Walter Map's text to read "Bello Loco", where "Bello Joco" is intended.[2] This is to make confusion worse confounded. Guischard de Beaujeu, according to the *Biographie universelle*, was flourishing in 1115, turned Cluniac monk and died in 1137. Guischard de Beaulieu was an Anglo-Norman writer of about the end of the twelfth century, who, like so many others, retired after a life in the world to the safe haven of a Benedictine cloister (l. 1312). The two persons are quite clearly distinct.

This confusion between Guischard de Beaujeu and Guischard de Beaulieu is not the only difficulty connected with the identity of Guischard the writer of the *Sermon*, and there is another that is more serious because more persistent. It was quite properly concluded by de la Rue, one of the earliest investigators into the subject, that he came from Beaulieu Priory in Bedfordshire, a cell of St. Albans. Now this Priory was always somewhat obscure. It was founded 1140–6 and a still earlier cell at Milbrook was removed and united with it to give it a better start, but it always seems to have been poor, struggling and with few

[1] *Biographia Britannica Literaria*, Anglo-Norman Period, pp. 132 ss.
[2] *De Nugis Curialium* (Oxford, 1914), p. 19.

inhabitants.   Finally it was decided to give it up, and between 1434 and 1464 it was reunited with St. Albans.   The name seems only to be commemorated today by a farm called Beadlow.[1] Obviously, it was not the sort of place where writers might be expected to flourish, but from its history it would seem that the first fifty years of its existence, when some effort was being made to colonise it from Milbrook and St. Albans itself, are the most likely to have been the most fruitful.   All are agreed that Guischard was a late twelfth-century writer.   His language, his versification and his subject all point to this conclusion.   Nevertheless, later writers, including Vising, have assumed that he came from the better known House of Beaulieu in Hampshire.   Even the latest editor of the text, who believes firmly in the twelfth-century date, subscribes to this opinion in an article he published some years after his edition had appeared.[2]   There are two objections to this view.   One is, that the Hampshire Beaulieu was Cistercian.   Gabrielson argued that Cistercians followed the Benedictine Rule.   So they did, but so did the monks and nuns of every other Western Order.   " A follower of the Rule of St. Benedict " is best applicable as a description of a Benedictine. In his edition, Gabrielson even misquotes the Abbé de la Rue, saying that he declared that Guischard belonged to the Cistercian Priory of Beaulieu.   At that point, Gabrielson does not seem to have been aware that there were two Beaulieus.[3]   Apart from this question of Order, there is another objection to the Hampshire Beaulieu.   It was not founded until 1204, and the buildings were not dedicated until 1246.   Although 1204 is very early in the thirteenth century, it is late for Guischard.   Gabrielson, in his article, is obliged to express a pious hope that there was some earlier religious House on the spot, but there is no evidence that anything had previously existed when King John devoted a portion of the New Forest to his new foundation.

[1] *V.C.H. Beds*, i. 351, ii. 321.
[2] A. Gabrielson, *Archiv für neuere Sprachen*, cxxviii (1912), p. 312.
[3] *Le Sermon de Guischard de Beaulieu* (Uppsala and Leipzig, 1909), p. lvii.

Guischard addresses his audience as " seignurs ", but was writing more particularly for a certain Dame Dionise (l. 1319). If the identity of this lady could be discovered, that would be decisive as to time and place, but unfortunately the name was far too popular in the twelfth and thirteenth centuries to be of much help. She is unlikely to have been a very well-known person, for her name has been suppressed in two of the three manuscripts, which is the reason why her existence was not suspected until the publication of Gabrielson's edition. Langtoft's chronicle provides a parallel case of the suppression of a patron's name. " Uns amis " has been substituted for " Schafeld ". The search for Dionysia may not have proved quite so fruitless as that for Schafeld has been, for there was a lady of that name, a neighbour both of St. Albans and of its cell Beaulieu, who may have been the one in question. She was the wife of Walter Hacon. In 1198 she and her husband, who owned lands in Hertfordshire and Bedfordshire, were involved in a lawsuit concerning lands in Bedfordshire which Dionysia must have brought into the family, since her presence was essential to the action. She fell ill, and the case was delayed on that account. In 1200 it was again reported by those sent to investigate her alleged illness that she was " languida ", that is, " suffering from an illness that is ground for essoin ".[1] Walter seems to have been alive at least until 1217, but the last entry concerning Dionysia which has found its way into print is in 1203. Perhaps the illness of 1200 was fatal; perhaps, too, it had turned her thoughts to serious matters and inspired a neighbouring monk to write for her a poem on the delusions of life in the world ; all this is pure conjecture, but the existence of a Dionysia, at the expected time and place, who provides an occasion for a sermon, is surely worth recording.[2]

---

[1] *Mediaeval Latin Word List* (O.U.P., 1934).

[2] The following entries refer to Walter Hacon :

Rotuli curiae Regis, i. 160, 165 (with Dionysia), 270, 292 (with Dionysia), 440 (with Dionysia), ii. 83, 84, 220 (with Dionysia).

Calendar of Curia Regis Rolls, i. 355 (with Dionysia), 451, ii. 142, 272 (with Dionysia), iii. 5, 230, 315.

According to Gabrielson, Guischard's sources included not only *St. Alexis*, the sermon *Grant mal fist Adam* and other French works, but English homiletic literature, Ælfric in particular. The relationship between Guischard and the English *Poema Morale* has yet to be worked out. If he was really well acquainted with English works, this is an interesting point. Anglo-Norman writers did not make much use, if any, of English sources after the twelfth century, though before that they seem to have read English. The name Guischard does not suggest English descent, and if he was well versed in English literature this fact is important. It may be pointed out that his use of occasional English words in French dress, even of the same words as occur in English translations of the common Latin sources, is not as conclusive as Gabrielson thinks of the use of the English as an intermediary. Even writers of French origin picked up a semi-English vocabulary with the greatest of ease. What is certain is that Guischard is reproducing the ideas which everybody shared at the end of the twelfth century. More interesting, perhaps, even than the resemblance of the *Sermon* to the *Poema Morale* is its resemblance to the *Vers* of Thibaud de Marly, an almost contemporary French writer, whose mother was a natural daughter of Henry I and was brought up in England. Late in life Thibaud became a Cistercian. Writing of the remarkably close resemblance between the two poems, the editor of the *Vers* declares : " On pourrait interpoler des tirades entières de l'un dans l'ouvrage de l'autre et aucun lecteur non averti ne s'apercevrait de la supercherie ".[1] Thibaud's poem is shorter

---

Abbrevatio Placitorum, 7 (with Dionysia), 23, 36.
Rotuli Clausarum, i. 326 b.
 (*N.B.*—More than once the clerks mixed up the names of the parties.)
Receipt Roll of Exchequer, p. 12.
 The Walter Hacon temp. Henry III (*Book of Fees*, i. 484, *Calendar of Ancient Deeds*, i, *Rotuli Hundredorum*, ii. 80 (Salop), *Excerpta ex Rotulis Finium*, ii. 217, 256), was probably the son of Walter and Dionysia.
 Richard Hakun and Denise, his wife, owned lands in Kent (*Calendar of Charter Rolls*, i. 459 (1257), *Excerpta ex Rotulis Finium*, ii. 162 (1253)).
 [1] Herbert King Stone, *Les Vers de Thibaud de Marly* (Paris, 1932), p. 70. Cf. *Les Œuvres de Guiot de Provins*, ed. John Orr (Manchester, 1915).

and better arranged than Guischard's, and is probably a little later. He introduces proper names in a way which foreshadows the satirical use of the " Ubi sunt " theme by Guiot de Provins in his *Bible*, which belongs to the beginning of the next century.

Guischard confines himself to the theme, eternally fascinating, of " Hora novissima, tempora pessima sunt, vigilemus ". Writing for some great lady living in the world, he is able, without feeling himself a prig, to point to himself as an example of one who had been able to detach himself from the worldly life he used to love. His is the mentality of St. Alexis. The title " Romanz " is justified by the form of the poem, which is cast in the form of a *chanson de geste*, with its *laisses* of alexandrines.

Last, but not least, the claim of yet another writer to be numbered amongst the monks of St. Albans will have to be considered by the future editor of his work. This is the twelfth-century romancer Thomas of Kent. The personality of this man is vague. Even his name has been the subject of dispute. Early Continental scholars imagined that he came from Caen, but there is no doubt that he wrote in Anglo-Norman and that his surname was Kent. His Christian name is still sometimes misquoted. The manuscript tradition varies between Thomas and Eustace. Paul Meyer [1] inclined to the view that his name was really Eustace, partly because there are already two Anglo-Norman romances, *Tristan* and *Horn*, ascribed to writers named Thomas, partly because he thought that Eustace was the more usual form in the manuscripts. Miss C. B. West [2] also plumps for Eustace on mathematical grounds. As a matter of fact, his name was obviously Thomas. In the first place, it has not been proved absolutely that the three romances are the work of three and not of two or even one. In the second, Paul Meyer and Miss West were mistaken in their arithmetic. In two of the manuscripts both

---

[1] [37.] P. Meyer, *Alexandre le Grand* (Paris, 1886), i. 283 ss. Edition in contemplation by Bateman Edwards.

[2] C. B. West, *Courtoisie in Anglo-Norman Literature* (Oxford, 1938), pp. 71, 72.

Thomas and Eustace occur; in one only Thomas is mentioned. The majority is not three to one in favour of Eustace as Paul Meyer thought, but eight to three in favour of Thomas, and there is one manuscript (unfortunately incomplete) which gives Thomas only, and none which gives Eustace alone. Lastly, the name Eustace is probably a scribal error which is easily accounted for, Eustace being the name of the author of the *Fuerre de Gadres*, an episode which was interpolated into Thomas's work.[1]

The establishing of a name does not give one much to go upon, unless that name can be traced in some record or other, and this, in the case of Thomas of Kent, has never been done. But from internal evidence it is clear that this writer had had a clerkly education, and that his intention was to retell the story of Alexander not for mere entertainment but for the moral lessons which might be drawn from it. Hence the new title " *Roman de Toute Chevalerie* ".[2] It may be that Thomas was not in orders and was putting his knowledge to worldly purposes. In support of this view Miss West quotes the line " Pur çoe ke jolif sui e ne gueres letré ", but this is little to set against the testimony of the work as a whole and would not be incompatible with the supposition that after a life in the world he had withdrawn to the shelter of the cloister.

The manuscripts themselves suggest that Thomas was a Benedictine. Of the three surviving fairly complete MSS., one is in the possession of a former Benedictine Library, now the Durham Chapter Library, though how and when it arrived there is unknown; a second is believed to have been executed at St. Albans; while the third was not only probably executed there, but is ornamented by two miniatures of the author dressed as a Black Monk.

This last is now in Paris, Bibliothèque Nationale, fonds français 24, 364. On the first folio, which contains the prologue, the

---

[1] These points were worked out by Johanna Weynand, *Der Roman de Toute Chevalerie des Thomas von Kent in seinem Verhältnis zu seinen Quellen* (Bonn, 1911).

[2] Cf. P. Meyer, *op. cit.*, and J. Weynand, *op. cit.*

author, meticulously clad in a Benedictine habit, is depicted seated in a chair, pen and scraper in hand, writing his book, which is displayed on a desk in front of him. On f. 31 b, the initial of the line

Qui geste volt conter, ou estoire traiter

is filled in by a miniature of the same monk, this time seated on a stone bench, reading from a large book held with both hands.

These miniatures have not escaped notice. The first was described by Amaury Duval, *Histoire littéraire*, xix. 675, but he said, erroneously, that the costume was of a "religieux bernardin". More interesting are the remarks of Le Grand d'Aussy (*Notices et extraits*, v. 122), " Je soupçonnerois même, d'après la miniature du début et celle du folio 31, où il est représenté en habit de moine noir, composant son ouvrage, qu'en effet il étoit religieux ; si dans deux autres miniatures (l'une fol : 50 ; l'autre fol : 44 v°, endroit où il se nomme) on ne le voyoit également en habit de couleur, ayant robe à chaperon avec manches pendantes ". This third miniature is not, however, intended for the author. There are several other pictures of men writing, and if they are considered in relation to the passages they illustrate, it will be seen that they are intended to represent the following persons :

On f. 36 c, Alexander's secretary.

On f. 44 d, (below the place where he names himself), the Latin author he is translating.

On f. 45 a, the secretary writing the " Épistre d'Alisandre " to Aristotle.

On f. 50 b, " Hieronimus the Historian " and Solinus.

In each case these scribes are depicted as venerable, bald-headed men in long gowns with hoods, and long tunics. The miniaturist seems to have had a vague idea that pagans would look like monks in coloured garments. The two pictures of a Black Monk are intended for the same person, every detail of face and attire is similar ; the others are of different people, with different faces and clothes.

There is one picture of a man writing in Cambridge, Trinity

College MS. O. 9, 34. At the rubric on f. 22 a, " La conclusion del
liuere Al. De maistre eustace ki translata cest liure ", is the
portrait of a bald-headed man wearing a green gown with hood,
sitting writing in a chair to which a desk is attached. This
miniature corresponds to the one of f. 44 d of the Paris MS. of a
man in a gray gown over a pink tunic, which is meant for the
author of the Latin original. As there are several quires missing
from the beginning of the Cambridge MS., there is no means of
knowing if there was once a miniature of the author on the first
page. This manuscript is thus described by Dr. M. R. James [1] :
" The work is excellent ; and the style of both drawing, colouring
and writing inclines me to hazard the conjecture that the birth-
place of the volume was St. Albans Abbey ". After epitomising a
MS. account of the Paris MS. by Paul Meyer, he goes on to say :
" This MS. closely resembles ours in the writing and the miniatures ". This might suggest that the two MSS. are in the same
hand, but this is not the case. The hand, illustration and arrangement of the Paris MS. are strongly reminiscent of MS. Cambridge
University Ee. 3, 59, " La Estoire de St. Ædward le Rei ", which
is of course also a St. Albans book, of about the mid-thirteenth
century. Dr. James [2] dated the Cambridge Alexander about 1250.

There is therefore a strong suggestion that Thomas of Kent
was a Benedictine, possibly of St. Albans itself. Unfortunately,
no monk of that name is known to have existed there, or at any
of its cells. The name is unlikely to have belonged to an inmate
of either of the Canterbury Houses, where it would have led to
confusion. It must not be forgotten that St. Albans was the home
of a Latin compilation about Alexander, made between 1146 and
1151. [3] The library must have been rich in Alexandrine material,
amongst which Thomas could find "l'estoire de l'almaire" (p. 222).

In the past there was much speculation over the possible
identity of Mestre Thomas who wrote the Romance of Horn, and

[1] Trinity College Cambridge Catalogue of the Western MSS. iii. 482.
[2] M. R. James, Roxburghe Club, 1920.
[3] Paul Meyer, op. cit. ii, ch. IV.

Thomas, the author of *Tristan*. It is generally concluded that they were not the same person. It is unlikely that the Thomas who wrote *Horn* is Thomas of Kent. Their writings bear no resemblance, and, for all that he styles himself " Mestre ", the *Horn* Thomas refers to a son at the end of his work, to whom a man of the erudition of Thomas of Kent, whether or not he was a monk, would hardly have confessed. There remains the possibility that Thomas of Kent wrote *Tristan*, a possibility which has hardly been discussed, chiefly because it was believed that the author of the *Roman de Toute Chevalerie* was named Eustace.

Now, however, that it is clear that he was called Thomas, the matter must be reopened. It is highly improbable that an English Benedictine could have written *Tristan*—*Alexandre* is as far as he is likely to have gone. If, therefore, Thomas of Kent was a Benedictine and author of the *Roman* and of *Tristan*, either the *Roman* is the work of his old age, when, like his old rival Denis Pyramus of St. Edmunds, he had retired from court, or *Tristan* is the work of a runaway monk. The former explanation is the more likely. It is true that surnames usually occur in early works, and that the Thomas of *Tristan* has none, but the rule is not a hard and fast one and so much of *Tristan* is lost that too much cannot be made of this fact.

But are there any reasons for thinking that these two Thomases might have been one, beyond the coincidence of name ? The answer can only be supplied by internal evidence, and the fragmentary nature of *Tristan* and the unpublished state of the *Roman de Toute Chevalerie* make comparison difficult. As far as can be gathered from the *Tristan* fragments published by Bédier for the Société des anciens textes français and from the study of the language of the *Roman de Toute Chevalerie* by H. Schneegans,[1] there is no objection to the identification on linguistic grounds, and Bédier and Schneegans attributed the objects of their respective studies to the end of the twelfth century, or at least the second half of it.

---

[1] *Zeitschrift für französiche Sprache und Literatur*, xxxi (1907), pp. 1 ss.

Tristan is of course far superior, being in fact one of the most outstanding poems in Old French. The penetration and passion, and the lyrical quality of the verse, have often been extolled. *Le Roman de Toute Chevalerie* is poor in these respects. But this may be explained. *Tristan* is a creative work, a revision of a diversity of tales, written in the new-fangled octosyllable. In the *Roman*, the writer was sticking more closely to his sources, and was employing the long line which bears to this day the name of the Worthy with whom it was already associated, and as a monk he would have to hold in check the inspiration which has made of *Tristan* one of the supreme songs of the world, and kindled a flame which was to warm the hearts of Gottfried von Strassburg and of Wagner. Like Denis Pyramus, Thomas may have retired from the world, but nothing would stop him writing. Denis Pyramus was fortunate in being provided with a suitable subject. Thomas had to find one, and he found it in the monastic bookcase.[1]   It was, therefore, respectable enough, but it was not Christian and required an apology. The later compiler of MS. Douce 299 explained that he wrote to combat " accidia " and to diminish the temptations which lead to vagrancy on the part of monks.[2]   Thomas wrote a Prologue :

> Mult par est icest(e) siecle dolenz e perilleus,
> Fors à icels qui servent le hault rei glorius
> Qui por nus delivra le seon sanc precius ;
> Si cum mestier nus est eiet mercit de nus !

(This world is sad and perilous save to those who serve the high and glorious King who shed His precious blood for us ; as is needful for us may He have mercy upon us.) However, some " delit " is permissible, and

> Un deduit ai choisi qi mult est delitus,
> As tristes confort e joie as dolerus

---

[1] P. Meyer, *op. cit.* i. 222.   The quotations which follow are all from the extracts printed in this book.

[2] P. Meyer, *op. cit.* ii. 65.

E assuagement as mals des amerus.
Deliter s'i poent homme ben chevalerus
E tuit ceo [*sic*] qi de romanz sunt coveitus.

(I have chosen a pastime which is very delightful, comfort to the sad and joy for the grieving, and assuagement for the pangs of lovers. Knightly men can please themselves with it, and all those who are desirous of romance.)

The echo is faint, but surely there is something about these lines which recalls the magic ending of *Tristan* :

Tumas fine ci sun escrit :
A tuz amanz saluz i dit,
As pensis e as amerus,
As emvius, as desirus,
As enveisiez e as purvers,
A tuz cels ki orunt ces vers.   (ll. 3125-30)

(Here Thomas ends his tale ; he greets in it all lovers, those melancholy and those in love, those desiring and those longing, those who are joyous and those who are distraught, all those who hear these lines.)

And later :

Pur essemple l'ai issi fait
E pur l'estorie embelir,
Que as amanz deive plaisir
E que par lieus poissent trover
Chose u se puissent recorder :
Aveir em poissent grant confort,
Encuntre change, encuntre tort,
Encuntre paine, encuntre plur,
Encuntre tuiz engins d'amur !

(I have done this for the sake of the example, and to beautify the tale, that it may please lovers, and that they may find something in it in places where they may be reminded of themselves. May they derive great comfort from it, against inconstancy and against injury, against grief, against tears, against all the wiles of love.)

The moralising tendency of Thomas, which here assorts so oddly with his subject, has often been observed. There was more

D

scope for a tendency of this kind in the *Roman de Toute Chevalerie.*
Both writers continue with a justification. After an allusion to
the " enviouse gent ", also condemned by Denis Pyramus,
Thomas of Kent adds :

> Si nuls d'els me reprent, seignurs, tant di à vous ;
> L'ume mesprent sovent en outre mal grevus.
> Mult par serreit li homme en ses fez eüreus
> Si à la fiée n'est repris des envious.
> Ore poet qui voelt oïr un vers merveillus
> D'Alexandre le rei. . . .

(If any of them reprove me, lords, I say this to you ; one often
does other than grievous wrong. A man would indeed be lucky
in his actions if from time to time he is not reproved by the
envious. Now he who wishes can hear a marvellous poem about
Alexander the King. . . .)

And the other Thomas in milder fashion :

> Si dit n'ai a tuz lor voleir,
> Le milz ai dit a mun poeir.

(If I have not said what pleases everyone, I have said the best I
could.) Thomas of Kent supplied his first book with an epilogue
in which he explains that he has followed his source faithfully :

> Mes beles paroles e ai mis nequedent. . . . .
> Pur plaisir as oianz est un atiffement.
> Home ne deit lang[ag]e traslater autrement
> Qui deï[s]t mot por mot trop irreit leidement.

(But I have added fair words nevertheless. . . . It is an ornament
to please the hearers. One ought not to translate language
otherwise. He who should say word for word would write in too
ugly a fashion.) It is here that he names himself :

> Qui [de] mun non demande, Thomas ai non de Kent ;
> E pur çoe me nom [joe] en cest enbrievement
> Ne voil qu'atre ait blasme de çoe k'a moi apent.

(If one asks about my name, Thomas it is, of Kent. And for this reason I name myself in this work, I do not wish another to have the blame for what concerns me.) The epilogue begins with these lines, which refer to the prologue :

> De Darie et d'Alix, ai di ces que [joe] sent
> Si cum joe vus premis [tut] el comencement.

(Of Darius and Alexander I have said what I am aware of, just as I promised you right in the beginning.)

The other Thomas similarly refers to his prologue, which unfortunately is not extant :

> E dit ai tute la verur
> Si cum jo pramis al primur.

(And I have said all the truth, just as I promised at the first.)

May not this be the same mind at work, the monk, in his old age, still making clumsy use of the devices with which, in his youth, he had thrilled the courts of kings, now reduced to tricks of the trade to catch the ears of the passing nobles in the monastic guest-house ?

If Thomas of Kent was really a monk, he obviously still felt the tug of the world and regret for the past, and if he was also the author of *Tristan*, what a tragedy not only for himself, but for all of us may lie behind the transformation. And what a commentary on what monastic life might do to poetic inspiration, that inspiration which was once again recognised at the Renaissance as being not a wile of the devil, but of divine origin.

IV

SOME BENEDICTINE MONKS AND NUNS

COMPARED with the two great Houses of Bury St. Edmunds and St. Albans, the rest of England has little to show in the way of works written by Benedictine monks. Elie de Winchester has already been mentioned as a translator of the *Distichs of Cato*, partly in tail-rhyme. He wrote probably early in the thirteenth century, and is now thought to be the original writer from whom two later revisions were made. From the fact that he called himself Danz, and describes himself as being of Winchester, it may be conjectured that he was a monk of the Cathedral Priory.

Burton Abbey is almost certainly the home of an anonymous *Life* of St. Modwenna [107]. This Celtic saint, whose *Life* is a conflation of the careers of at least two different people of more or less the same name, was the patroness of the Abbey at Burton, a place which has narrowly escaped being known as Modwenstow. Geoffrey, Abbot from 1114–51, wrote a *Life* in Latin, which was followed fairly closely with a few additions by a translator writing in the early thirteenth century. It seems unreasonable to do otherwise than suppose that this is an interesting example of the *Life* of a patron saint being first written in Latin by an inmate of a monastery and subsequently rendered into the vernacular by another. The Anglo-Norman *Life* is written in a form which is very rare, and consists of 2035 monorhymed octosyllabic quatrains. Most saints' *Lives* are written in octosyllabic couplets, though, as has been seen, alexandrine tirades and tail-rhyme stanzas are occasionally used. The *Life* has lately been

44

edited.[1] A comparable case of patriotism occurs at Peterborough. The compressed translation [63] of Abbot Hugh Candidus' *Chronicle*, published by Sparke in 1723 from a Cotton manuscript since burnt, is almost undoubtedly the work of a later monk. This time the hero is the foundation itself, and the form is rough alexandrines in assonance.

From Canterbury come two chronicles. In the fourteenth century John of Canterbury wrote his *Polistorie* either at Christ Church Priory or at St. Augustine's.[2] Much earlier, about 1274, Christ Church may have produced two genealogies of British and English Kings which have been ascribed to Peter of Ickham.[3] It is not at all clear whether Peter of Ickham actually wrote this work, or whether he merely bequeathed a volume containing it to the library, for he seems to have owned a number of books which found their way there. Glover identified this chronicle with *Le Livere de Reis de Brittanie et le Livere de Reis de Engleterre* which he edited in the Rolls Series, but even this identification is uncertain. The work he printed is an unusually deadly prose abridgment of the *Brut* and the common Latin chronicles, with a few original additions. It is, in fact, just the kind of thing a monk might concoct out of the chronicles and annals available to him, and that is its chief interest. The two continuations of this chronicle, known as the " Wroxham " and the " Sempringham " Continuations, though they are products of religious houses, hardly come into the scope of this present inquiry, being straightforward accounts of contemporary happenings which can scarcely be classed as literature.

Curiously enough, York as well as Canterbury produced a chronicle whose exact significance it is difficult to assess. This is the *Anonimalle Chronicle* of St. Mary's, York. It is perhaps the only work of the kind to be written in French, not Latin, and the

[1] Ed. A. T. Baker and A. Bell (Anglo-Norman Text Society, vii, 1947).

[2] [376.] *Hist. litt.* xxviii. 480 ss., Duffus Hardy, iii, No. 576.

[3] [298.] M. R. James, *Ancient Libraries of Canterbury and Dover* (Cambridge, 1903).

reason for this seems to be that it, too, is a " Continuation ", this time of the ordinary *Brut* chronicle. It is contemporary authority for the years 1376–81.[1]

One of the earliest of Anglo-Norman texts, the *Life* of St. Brendan [10], is probably the work of a Benedictine, but a Benedictine of an unknown House. This poem is one of the most attractive of all the saints' *Lives* which were ever written in French, and had a considerable vogue on the Continent. Part of the attraction lies in the subject, the skilful welding of the missionary's historic journeys with Celtic mythological wanderings and half-remembered, half-invented adventures in the Arctic seas. To this day Americans are to be found who will give St. Brendan credit for the discovery of the American Continent, while others are more interested in his glimpse of Jan Mayen Land. But much is due also to the Anglo-Norman writer, for his simple yet eloquent style, his narrative skill and sense of drama, his power over words and use of sea-terms, and the manner in which he handles his peculiar system of versification. However fantastic the adventure, however unpractical the hero, however technical the details of the voyage, the writer keeps his head, he contrives never to be boring, and this is something remarkable in the Middle Ages, when dullness was a merit and not a vice. Unfortunately, the authorship of this delightful poem is a mystery. There is indeed a clue, but the meaning of it is lost. The line " li apostoiles Danz Benedeiz " is in its way as great a stumbling-block as the more famous " Ci falt la geste que Turoldus declinet ". The words suggest that the author was a Benedictine monk, for " Dan " was already in use as an ecclesiastical title, and the mysterious " apostoiles " may be an adjective meaning one who follows the apostolic or regular way of life, though its usual meaning is " pope ", as a substantive. This is as far as the editor, E. G. R. Waters,[2] would allow himself to go.

---

[1] Edited by V. H. Galbraith (Manchester, 1927).
[2] *The Anglo-Norman Voyage of St. Brendan by Benedeit* (Oxford, 1928), p. xxvii.

It may be added that the name Benedeit may have been assumed in honour of the Founder of the Rule.   Beneit is also the name of the St. Albans writer of the *Life* of Thomas à Becket.   *St. Brendan* is dedicated to Adeliza, second queen of Henry I, a patroness of letters whose name will recur.   The writer may therefore have been a member of the Royal foundation of Westminster, or of King Henry's own foundation of Reading, in which Adeliza took the greatest interest.

Lastly, it must not be forgotten that St. Brendan is a Benedictine saint, and that, legend apart, he was once upon a time a real abbot.   There are only two churches in England dedicated to him, both in places connected directly with the saint, who has given his name to the settlements as well as the churches.   These are Brendon in Devon and Brancepeth in Durham.[1]   The names of the chapel dedications of Reading are not known, and the plan of the church there can only be reconstructed with difficulty. Although consideration of monastic writings leads to the conclusion that a patron saint was the most likely to be honoured with a *Life*, and in consequence the first step to be taken when dealing with an anonymous *Life* is to hunt for a corresponding church or chapel dedication, there is no need to carry the process too far.   Queens could ask for what they wanted, and at times the monasteries were involved in a wave of universal sentiment : hence all the *Lives* of Thomas à Becket, inspired by horror and indignation.   The Latin *Life* of St. Brendan was much beloved. Dating back possibly to the ninth century, certainly to the tenth, when the text was already obscured by corruptions,[2] it cannot possibly have excited Adeliza of Louvain as a novelty.   The immediate occasion for this version must, therefore, remain as deep a mystery as the authorship for the present.   Yet everything seems to point to a Benedictine writer.

Even allowing for the loss of much, and the failure to identify

---

[1] F. Arnold-Forster, *Studies in Church Dedications* (1899), ii. 39, 40.
[2] Waters, p. lxxxii.

much more, it is impossible to escape the conclusion that Bury and St. Albans were more important than other monasteries as producers of works in Anglo-Norman, and it is interesting to note that these are the very monasteries singled out by Professor David Knowles [1] as having had some small share of the twelfth-century renaissance.   Latin and French were not rivals, but partners.   Where much Latin was written, some French may be expected, but where there was no Latin, it is unlikely that French was used as a substitute.   There is, however, one possibility, that in nunneries French was used rather than Latin, and this possibility, therefore, falls to be examined.

NUNS

It must be remembered that in the later Middle Ages women were not given to writing at all.   Marie de France and the much later Christine de Pisan are the only two well-known writers in French.   They were not, however, illiterate, and, according to the romances, it was the damsels whose duty it was to read aloud in aristocratic households.[2]   In nunneries French became more and more the language for all purposes.   Every writer upon monastic life in England is struck by the contrast between the state of things in Saxon and early Norman times and the later period.   It is a far cry from the nuns who embellished their Obituary Lists with passable Latin hexameters to the nuns who were permitted by their Bishop to learn a Latin without flexions, a desperate expedient indeed.   In the fourteenth century Bishops seem to have abandoned the struggle and to have used nothing but French in their dealings with nuns.   Indeed, until the mid-fourteenth century French seems to have been the only language known in convents.[3]   This is probably the explanation of the translation into French of the *Ancrene Riwle*, if indeed it is a translation.   If it was written in English for a group of twelfth-

---

[1] *The Monastic Order in England* (Cambridge, 1940), p. 502.
[2] H. J. Chaytor, *From Script to Print* (Cambridge, 1945), p. 103.
[3] Cf. Eileen Power, *Medieval English Nunneries* (Cambridge, 1922), pp. 237, 247, 248.

century recluses, it might have been turned into French for nuns and possibly other great ladies. For the nunneries were aristocratic, and even the middle class was only gradually admitted in numbers.

If the nuns read or wrote anything, therefore, one would have expected it to be Anglo-Norman. Convents, however, seem to have owned hardly any books.[1] This question of nuns' libraries is one which will come up later. Meanwhile it does something to explain the remarkable dearth of books written by nuns, though why girls who, if they had been at home, would have been reading romances to their families, should have ceased to read because they had entered the cloister is a mystery. It is not as though they had been brought up out of touch with the world, for many, if not most, of them had been wives and mothers before they became nuns.

The matter, however, is not so grave as was thought until recently. Eileen Power,[2] for instance, only knew of one French work written by a nun, the well-known *Life* of St. Catherine of Alexandria by Clemence of Barking.

One nun-authoress is perhaps more extraordinary than no authoresses at all, and it is therefore not surprising to find that other writers have turned up since. There is also the fascinating possibility that Marie de France was Abbess of Shaftesbury, but this is a thorny subject and best left out of account for the present. Barking was one of the oldest and greatest of Houses for women in England. About 1150–60 a nun named Clemence wrote there her *Life* of St. Catherine [11].[3] The convent was dedicated to the Virgin Mary, but there is nothing unexpected about a nun writing a *Life* of the most celebrated of Virgin Martyrs, whose popularity may be measured by the countless uses of the catherine wheel, her emblem, to this very day. The work is competent, even if it misses the height of inspiration to which Denis Pyramus and the unknown author of *St. Brendan* could attain, and was frequently copied. Some time later another work issued from

---

[1] Eileen Power, *op. cit.* pp. 241, 242.
[2] *Op. cit.* p. 239.   [3] Edited by Jarnic (Prague, 1894).

Barking. This is a *Life* of Edward the Confessor [127], which also seems to have enjoyed a certain amount of popularity, for not only does it survive in two manuscripts, one of them the inevitable Welbeck collection, but someone paid it the compliment of turning it into prose. This *Life* falls into the conventional two parts, a Life and an account of miracles. It was translated from the Latin at Barking by a nun who refuses to name herself, for her name was not worthy to be written in a book where such a holy name was inscribed (as that of St. Edward). The work is not to be despised on the grounds that the translator was a woman. All this looks as though the writer was not the same person as Clemence, and as though women writers are uncommon and unexpected. One of the miracles was told to the writer by a nun who was still living at the Abbey. The author speaks as if she herself was not one of the seniors, and on those grounds alone it would be reasonable to conclude that she was a younger woman than Clemence. The language of the two *Lives* has been the subject of an investigation which bears out this view, but unfortunately the results are locked up in an unpublished thesis. One curious detail is that both *Lives* end with the same doxology. The second nun was therefore either copying Clemence, or conforming to a Barking custom.[1]

A third saint's *Life* may be due to a nun. This is the thirteenth-century *Life* of St. Audrey [2] which is preserved, so far as is known, only in the Welbeck MS. The writer names herself " Marie, Pur ce ke soie remembree ". She used as source a redaction of Bede's *Life* by Thomas, a twelfth-century Benedictine of Ely. St. Audrey had been Abbess of Ely, and it is possible that Marie was a Benedictine nun, but not of Ely, as Karl suggests, for the last of the race were massacred there in A.D. 870. The short extracts printed are not long enough to justify any

---

[1] Cf. M. D. Legge, *Medium Ævum*, vi (Feb. 1937), pp. 31 ss., " The Vatican Life of Edward the Confessor ", and edition by O. Södergård (Uppsala, 1948).

[2] L. Karl, " Notice sur un MS. français de la bibliothèque du duc de Portland à Welbeck ", *Revue des Langues romanes*, liv. 216. Cf. unpublished thesis by J. A. Malone (Sheffield).

speculation as to Marie's identity, but there is of course the possibility that she, too, came from Barking. She is, however, more likely to have been an Austin Canoness.

Three nuns may not seem very many, though it is a much more respectable number than Eileen Power's one. If it has taken so many years to find them, there may yet be others still unknown to us. Yet when it is considered that only two French-women have found a place in histories of mediaeval French literature, and that so many Houses of Benedictine monks in England seem to have produced no writers in French at all, the position does not seem quite so disgraceful. None of these three women were the equals of Denis Pyramus or the unknown poet of *St. Brendan*, as has already been remarked of Clemence, but they are at least fit to rank with second-rate men writers like Simon of Walsingham, and if they had not declared their identity no one would have suspected that they were women. In fact, the *Life* of St. Edward had long been known in a superficial way without the authorship being discovered, and without anyone remarking that there was anything peculiar about it. So, many other anonymous saints' *Lives* may have been written by women. Perhaps the most curious fact of all is that so far no one seems to have unearthed a Continental nun-authoress.[1]

None of the three English nuns wrote later than the thirteenth century. This is not so much because they were women, as because they were nuns. It will be noticed that none of the Benedictine men wrote a saint's *Life* after that period. This is partly because the fashion for the verse *Life* passed, but partly because of the rise of the schools. The decay of literature in nunneries was dependent upon its decay in the monasteries. The monasteries were killed as the sole centres of culture by the universities, and they dragged the nunneries down with them. The nuns were even worse off than the monks, for Gloucester College had no feminine counterpart.

---

[1] One Beguine writer is known, E. Bechmann, "Drei dits de l'âme", *Zeitschrift für romanische Philologie*, xiii (1889), p. 56.

V

CISTERCIANS AND A TEMPLAR

T HE list of Benedictine writers now completed numbers some fifteen. Consideration of it will shew, however, that the House counted for more than the Order and the individual than the House. Those reformed Benedictines, the Cistercians, might have been expected to have written something when one thinks of their record in France. There they pounced upon the Grail story and made it a vehicle for their own peculiar doctrine of grace. They also produced one writer of their own, Guillaume de Deguilleville, who wrote allegory in quantity though hardly of quality. His work is also the appropriation of other men's goods, for his three *Pilgrimages* are inspired by the *Roman de la Rose*, and he plagiarises to an extent which is remarkable even in the Middle Ages, when plagiarism was a recognised form of art. Intolerably dull as he is, he left his mark, and Lydgate and possibly even Bunyan are witnesses to his success.

In England things were different, and the Cistercians form a useful object-lesson against the hasty assumption that Anglo-Norman literature is part of Mediaeval French, and bound to follow the same lines. In France the Cistercians remained the " unco guid " of the Regular Clergy, but in England, through circumstances which they doubtless felt were beyond their control, they turned into highly successful sheep farmers. They did not neglect in consequence all the arts, and their excess profits went to ornament the Yorkshire Dales with the splendid edifices, all against the rule, which are their memorial. But they were not interested in literature. They could write, it is true, chronicles and some oddments such as Henry de Saltry's *St. Patrick's Purgatory*, but in general they were more interested in producing parchment than in writing upon it. One writer has crept into Vising's bibliography on rather slender grounds. This is the monk Simon of Waverley, who had copied a manuscript for the sister-house of nuns at Wintney, and added a little personal letter in French verse on his own account. These few lines are more interesting as shewing that the everyday tongue of monks and nuns was French than as an example of Anglo-Norman literature.

One other Anglo-Norman writer may be suspected of having been a Cistercian. One of the versions of the *Vision of St. Paul*,[1] a poem in octosyllabic couplets, was by a man named Adam of Ross. Presumably he was an ecclesiastic of sorts, for he says of himself : " Jeo sui serf Deu Adam de Ros " (l. 414). Now Adam, like Thomas of Kent, was once thought to have been a Norman, for there is a place near Caen called Ros, but again there is no doubt that he was an Anglo-Norman writer. One of the MSS. which contains his poem (Cotton Vespasian A VII) also contains the *Ipomedon* of Hue de Roteland, a self-declared Herefordshire writer. In this copy are allusions to Hereford which do not occur in all the MSS. of this romance, and on these very slender grounds it has been concluded that the Ross in question was Ross-on-Wye. However, this is not now so certain. Mr. J. C. Russell discovered a monk of the name belonging to the Cistercian House of Dunbrody in Leinster who was flourishing in the year 1279.[2]

There is no proof whatever of his having been the author of the *Vision of St. Paul*, but in favour of the identification are the name, the status, and the fact that the story might have some appeal in the land of St. Patrick's Purgatory, which was exciting interest among Cistercians at about this time. The *Vision*, too, is

---

[1] [17.] L. E. Kastner, " The Vision of St. Paul ", *Zeitschrift für französische Sprache und Literatur*, xxix (1906), p. 274.

[2] *Dictionary of Writers of the Thirteenth Century in England* (Special Supplement 3 to the Bull. of the Inst. of Hist. Research, 1936). *Cal. Docs. Rel. Ireland, 1252–84*, p. 305.

written for " Vus ki estes a Deu vouez ". If the identification is accepted, it disposes of any connection between the text and Herefordshire. Dunbrody was founded by Hervey de Montmorency, Strongbow's successor. It lies on the highway leading from a port founded by either Strongbow or his daughter, which was named Ross, later Old Ross. Both Abbey and port were Anglo-Norman colonies. Obviously the Dunbrody Adam came from this Ross, a fact that Mr. Russell overlooked. Anglo-Norman was used, naturally, in the Anglo-Norman settlements in Ireland just as it was used in England. Anglo-Norman documents written in Ireland survive ; in all likelihood there was an Anglo-Norman literature also, and, as will be seen later, there is a possibility that an Irish-born friar was another important writer in French.

No Cistercian nuns seem to have written anything, and the only nuns other than Benedictines who may have been writers are the nuns of the Cluniac House of Delapré, Northants. A prose chronicle produced by this House has been edited by Mr. Denholm Young.[1] It is hardly literature, being merely an attempt to prove that the earldom of Huntingdon was held of the King of Scots and not of the King of England, a point of importance to " les dames " at Delapré because the Earl of Huntingdon was their patron. This chronicle is of great historical value and has the additional advantage that it can be dated with reasonable certainty. It must have been written in or just after 1237, but unfortunately is only known today in one of Sir William Dugdale's transcripts. Mr. Denholm Young assigns the composition of this narrative to a nun, but it is just possible that it was written for the Abbey by a male chaplain or man-of-business.

TEMPLARS

Thus it appears that in the production of Anglo-Norman texts in monasteries it is a case of the Benedictines first and the rest nowhere, but as a postscript to this very tentative list of

---

[1] *Bodleian Quarterly Record*, vi (1931), pp. 225 ss.

monks and nuns belonging to other Orders, there may be placed the name of a remarkable writer, the sole representative of the Military Orders. Here at least we are on firm ground. This prolific author has considerately left us his name, his description, the name of his House and a list of three out of four of his works. He names himself " Henri d'Arci, frere del temple Salemun ", and says that he wrote " Al temple de la Bruere ". The d'Arcis were a Lincolnshire family, patrons of the Templars, and one of their number, Brother Henry d'Arci,[1] was an important member of the Order between 1160 and 1180. Temple Bruer is in Lincoln-shire. It is unlikely that there was another Henry d'Arci who was a Templar, and in consequence the mid-thirteenth-century date suggested by Kastner for one of his works is too late. Paul Meyer also considered him to be a thirteenth-century writer, either of the first or second half of the century. These mistaken opinions are useful as proving how impossible it is to date Anglo-Norman works on linguistic grounds alone, especially when they are only known in later copies.

Henri d'Arci's four works are all translations, written in swinging alexandrines, rhyming in pairs. The same rhyme, however, is often repeated many times. He probably began with a version of the *Vitae Patrum*, which he translated :

> Nient pur les clers mes pur la laie gent,
> Que par le rumanz le entendent uniement.

(Not for the clerks but for the lay folk, that they may understand it right through in French.) This was followed by a *Life* of Thaïs, drawn from the same source, written partly for the " freres de la maisun ". In the epilogue to this poem he declares himself willing to write any number of other things, if desired, but that for the moment " voil un poi reposer ". However, in the next line he repents, and says that before stopping he will treat of the

[1] [111-14.] Paul Meyer, *Notices et extraits*, xxxv. 140 ss. ; Kastner, *Modern Language Review*, i (1906), p. 269. Cf. Russell, *Dictionary* and *Modern Philology*, xxviii (1931), p. 258, and B. A. Lees, *Records of the Templars in England* (1935), pp. 209, 246, 247. Edition in preparation by R. C. D. Perman.

coming of Antichrist, and then, by the grace of the Holy Ghost, of the pains which Paul the Apostle saw in hell. This he duly proceeded to do, and it is not known whether the pause which then ensued gave him courage to carry out his promise and rattle out any more of his fluent alexandrines. Whether he did or not, he had already written sufficient to be classed as one of the major Anglo-Norman writers, and now that his work can be dated on external evidence, he has become more important than ever. There is something very attractive about this gentleman, who more than anyone else appears to take his readers into his confidence. He is also humble, not with a mock humility, but with conviction. He has a splendid independence. Some chapters of his source he had no hesitation in leaving out, " Ces en qui je ne vi geres d'utilite ". This is interesting. Most mediaeval writers whatever their actual policy profess extreme veneration for the " ancien geste ", especially if it is written in the magic Latin language. Then he asks neither for gold nor silver, esteem nor praise, his reward will come at the Judgment Day. This is rather different from the usual formula asking for the readers' prayers. He does not attempt to wean his public from the love of romances, he simply tells a story and informs his hearers that it will do them good to listen to it, especially if they pay attention. By noticing these details it is possible to obtain a clearer idea of what a monkish writer was like. At first, the differences between the individual writers obscure the fact that they are fundamentally alike. Henri d'Arci lacks the quality of a Benedeit, a Denis Pyramus or a Matthew Paris, but he does possess a humanity which is foreign to all of them, and the contrast between them forms a useful introduction to other classes of religious writers, the Canons and the Friars.

VI

CANONS AND A CANONESS

THE Austin Canons were originally founded as associations of working clergy living together under a Rule. The Rule, however, from being the servant of the Canons rapidly turned into their master, and by the end of the twelfth century there was very little to distinguish a Canon's life from that of a Benedictine monk. Yet there remained a fundamental difference. All Canons were ordained priests, they were not enclosed, and they were mostly engaged upon some useful work such as preaching, lecturing or writing. Only gradually did the custom grow up of ordaining monks; they were always enclosed, and their principal exercise was the *Opus Dei.*

It is therefore to be expected that the Black Canons will have written quite as much in French as monks, if not more, that the predominance of certain Houses will not be so marked, and that the kind of thing they chose to write about will be more varied.

The earliest Anglo-Norman writer among the Canons was probably a member of a foundation whose history is that of the whole system in miniature.[1] In the year 1092 the sheriff of Cambridge and his wife made provision for a Prior and six Canons to serve the already existing church of St. Giles there, endowing them with churches and tithes. The churches were in the neighbourhood and the idea was, apparently, that the Canons should serve both their own and these outlying churches, but

---

[1] Cf. J. W. Clark, *The Observances in Use at the Augustinian Priory of St. Giles and St. Andrew at Barnwell* (Cambridge, 1897); W. H. Frere, " The Early History of Canons Regular as illustrated by the Foundation of Barnwell Priory ", *Fasciculus Joanni Willis Clark Dicatus* (Cambridge, 1909).

E

this state of things did not last long.   In 1112 a second founder
added to their endowments, and the Canons moved to a more
convenient spot, Barnwell, on the outskirts of the town, where a
spring provided a water supply.   The place had been the site of
a hermitage dedicated to St. Andrew.   At once they began to
build themselves a fresh church, which was not to be a parish,
but a conventual church.   Like the monks, the Canons were
beginning to adopt the vicious system of " sweating " vicars to
carry out their parochial duties, though they seem always to have
obtained leave to serve parishes more easily than monks.[1]   The
new church was consecrated in 1190 and given the double dedication to St. Giles and St. Andrew in commemoration of its
history, and thenceforth the Canons proceeded to celebrate two
patronal feasts yearly.

It so happens that one of the best of the saints' *Lives* written
in Anglo-Norman, or for that matter in French, is the late
twelfth-century *Life* of St. Giles.[2]   From every point of view this
is an excellent work.   The language and style are attractive, the
author possessed a lively imagination and improved upon his
rather dry Latin original, and the subject gave him scope, St.
Giles, like St. Brendan, being one of those fortunate saints whose
lives are stranger than fiction.   The *Life*, like that of St. Brendan,
is characterised by a love of technical vocabulary, in this case not
only of sailing but of hunting as well.   It was probably written
between 1170 and 1200.

Near the end of the poem the author prays :

> Sun cher seignur
> Ke il par la sue dulçur
> Nus doinst cele veie tenir
> Par quei poissum a lui venir,
> E al chanoine sace gré
> Ki s'est peiné e travaillé
> De ceste vie translater.   (ll. 3757 ss.)

---

[1] Cf. R. A. R. Hartridge, *History of Vicarages in the Middle Ages* (Cambridge, 1930),
pp. 164 ss.

[2] [15.] Edited by G. Paris and A. Bos (S.A.T.F., 1881).

(His dear Lord that by His sweetness He may grant us to follow that way by which we may reach Him, and be gracious to the Canon who has not spared himself trouble and torment to translate this life.) There can therefore be no doubt that he was a Canon, and though it is left uncertain whether he was regular or secular, the probabilities are that he was a regular. He continues :

> Il ne quert pas sun nun celer :
> Gwillame ad nun de Bernevile,
> Ki par amur Deu e Seint Gile
> Emprist cest labur e cest fès.

(He does not seek to hide his name. William it is, of Bernevile, who through the love of God and of St. Giles undertook this labour and this burden.) In fact, he had already let the secret out :

> Gwillames dit de Bernevile
> K'en treis jurs vindrent a Marsile. (ll. 1039, 1040).

(William says, of Bernevile, that they came to Marseilles in three days.)

The editors of the text were convinced that Guillaume lived and wrote in England, partly because of his archaic style and the mixture of conservatism and incorrectness which distinguishes his language, partly because the only manuscript known to them is English, and partly because the only literary influence of this poem was upon the inevitable Lydgate. They naturally concluded that Berneville was the name of the place in Normandy from which his family was derived. In 1925, however, Ezio Levi [1] made the brilliant suggestion that Berneville represents Barnwell. It is indeed tempting to accept this identification. The poem might have been written in connection with the dedication of the new church in 1190. There were at least two Canons at Barnwell named William at about this time. William of Devon was elected the sixth Prior in 1208 and died in 1213. He was succeeded by the sacrist, William of Bedford, who, for some reason

---

[1] "Troveri ed Abbazie", *Archivio storico italiano*, lxxxiii (1925), pp. 65 ss.

unknown, died a few days after his election. These two men were probably much of an age. The circumstances of St. Giles's life in the grotto beside the spring, upon which the author loved to dwell, could not have failed to evoke in the minds of those who knew Barnwell as it was then, the former hermit of St. Andrew's and the Bairn's Spring ; nor the lavish foundation of the monastery in Provence, the erection of the new abode of the Canons. There can, however, be no question of proof here. It may be objected, too, that there is no justification for thinking that Barnwell could have been transformed into Bernevile— rhyming with Gile and Marsile. Unfortunately, no case of the name Barnwell occurring in a French document has so far turned up. The usual Latin forms are Barnewelle, Berenwelle or Brenwelle. The " -vile " according to the rhymes represents something which in Francien would have an " L mouillé ", but " vile " meaning " town " also rhymes with " Marsile " in this text (ll. 1045, 1060), and this rhyme is the more peculiar since the correct form of Marseilles would have been Marseille and not Marsille. " Bernevile ", therefore, in Guillaume's speech, may have represented something in between " Bernevile " and " Berneveille ", so that it is impossible to state that Bernevile does not stand for Barnwell.[1]

The Priory today is represented by a structure lying like a stranded ship in a sea of cabbage-patches and small grey-brick houses in one of the least attractive parts of modern Cambridge. One of the women's colleges runs a settlement there. It is odd to reflect that these young women may in some ways be continuing the work of a poet in whose eyes the neighbourhood conjured up visions of St. Giles and the miraculous hind.

Nowhere does Guillaume state that St. Giles was his patron, but he places great faith in the prayers of " seint Gile le bon barun " (l. 3770). The work was undertaken " Par amur Deu e Seint Gile " (l. 3766). It was written, naturally, to be read aloud —" D'un dulz escrit orrez la sume " (l. 1), " Oez, signurs,

---

[1] Cf. Introduction, *op. cit.* p. xxxii.

miracle grant " (l. 3441). The last line has a picturesque touch—
" Amen dites tut envirun ". It is certain that the author was a
Canon of sorts, even if he was not a Canon of Barnwell, and yet
there is nothing to distinguish this work in kind from the *Lives*
of St. Edmund, St. Faith and St. Alban. It is otherwise with
the later works of the English Canons.

Next in order of date comes a writer to whom both a locality
and a date can definitely be assigned. Angier was a Canon of
St. Frideswide's, the Priory that succeeded a nunnery and
ultimately evolved into the hybrid foundation of Christchurch.
His works [108] survive in one solitary manuscript which is
almost certainly autograph. In the year 1212 he was a subdeacon
and had been seven years a Canon. In this same year he must
have been ordained priest. The name Angier was not common.
Professor Pope deduced [1] from his language that he himself may
have been born in the Province of Anjou, but that he had passed
so much of his life in England that the accents of his youth had
become assimilated to those of the people amongst whom he
dwelt. He seems also to have adopted their feelings, as some of
his additions to the famous account of Augustine's mission to
England shew. Not only is he careful to mention that Paulinus
afterwards became what he calls Archbishop of York, but he
opens a chapter with the lines :

> Uimes vos dierrei des Engleis,
> As quels Deus dont victoire e peis !
> Com par Gregoire e ses vertuz
> A la Deu fei sont convertuz. (*Dialogues*, ll. 1867 ss.)

(Henceforth I will tell you about the English, to whom God
grant victory and peace ! How through Gregory and his virtues
they were converted to God's faith.)

Angier, like Guillaume de Berneville, wrote the kind of text
that a monk might have written. He completed his first task, a
translation of the *Dialogues* of St. Gregory, in about 24,000 octo-

---

[1] *Étude sur la langue de frère Angier* (Oxford and Paris, 1904).

syllables, in 1212. He was inspired to write because he was
distressed to find that stories of Arthur of Britain and songs of
Charlemagne were more popular than the Gospels, and that
jongleurs were more listened to than St. Peter or St. Paul. Unlike
Guillaume de Berneville, Angier was one of the dull, conscientious
type of writers. It is interesting to compare the two authors'
handling of dialogue. Guillaume de Berneville obtains an effect
of liveliness by splitting up his lines between the speakers, a
device used also by the anonymous author of the *Jeu d'Adam*,
while Angier never breaks up a line and his dialogue is in consequence artificial and monotonous. Like Marie de France, Angier
covers himself in advance against the attacks of envious critics
and rivals. He does not care for them, for he feels that he
is divinely inspired. The mediaeval conception of inspiration
differs from the Platonic, as the example of Angier shews.

Eighteen months after he had completed his translation of the
Dialogues, Angier added to it a translation of the *Life* of St.
Gregory. This occupies some 3000 lines. Unless he worked
very much more slowly, or unless there was a considerable pause
before he began this second task, it looks as though his work on
the *Dialogues* must have occupied most of Angier's first seven
years at St. Frideswide's.

There seems no particular reason why Angier should have
chosen to translate the works and life of Gregory the Great. In
this way his translations may perhaps be characterised as being
rather more pointless than those of the Benedictines whom he
resembles. Indeed, his writings today have only one merit, they
survive in an autograph manuscript, and he took the precaution
of signing and dating them. They seem to have achieved no
popularity, they may never have been copied or circulated, and
the solitary manuscript probably lay forgotten on the shelves
until the Dissolution. As will be seen, the very Canons themselves seem to have ignored it.[1]

---

[1] Cf. P. Meyer, *Romania*, xii. 145 ss. ; T. Cloran, *The Dialogues of Gregory the Great
translated into Anglo-Norman Verse by Angier* (Strassburg, 1901).

Soon after Angier was writing at St. Frideswide's, it is possible that a Canon of the neighbouring House of Oseney was at work upon that curious mixture of genealogical history, adventure and mysticism, the *Romance of Guy of Warwick*, for one of the Earls of Warwick, heirs of the d'Oyly family, founders and patrons of Oseney. The romance was probably composed between 1232 and 1242.[1]

Before the next writer who may be classed as a Black Canon had appeared on the scene, much water had flowed under the bridges. On the one hand, the laity were clamouring for encyclopaedic knowledge ; on the other, the clergy were only too anxious to satisfy them as far as religion was concerned. For in 1215 the Fourth Lateran Council had issued its decrees, including one, the twenty-first, laying down that it was the duty of all Christians to confess and communicate once a year, and ever since the Archbishops and Bishops of England had been busy amplifying and giving effect to this injunction. It was all finally summed up by the Franciscan, John Pecham, in his " Lay Folk's Catechism " of 1281. As a result of the Fourth Lateran, the Black Canons were holding frequent general Chapters from 1217 onwards,[2] and doubtless they were anxious to help forward the proposed reforms in other ways.

So the stage was set for the appearance of one of the most well-meaning but stupendously dull writers in Anglo-Norman, best-known, by what is probably a misnomer, as Peter of Peckham. In the York Chapter Library manuscript of one of his works it is stated that the text was begun at Newstead by Guildford and finished in Oxford in the year 1267. The Prologue is introduced in this manuscript by the drawing of an ecclesiastic writing at a desk, labelled " Autor ". The manuscript has naturally been claimed as autograph, but unfortunately this

---

[1] [212.] See Alfred Ewert, *Gui de Warewic* (Class. fr. du M.A., 1932), 1. iii-vii. But note that Professor Ewert invariably refers to the inhabitants of the Abbey as " moines ".

[2] M. Gibbs and J. Lang, *Bishops and Reform, 1215–72* (London, 1934), pp. 149-50.

cannot be proved, and consequently it remains doubtful whether the colophon refers to the author or the scribe, though the probabilities are that it refers to the former. There was a House of Austin Canons at Newstead, and so it is generally held that Peter was a Canon there who moved to Oxford to attend the Schools, for he is credited with a Master's Degree, though his name cannot be traced amongst early graduates either of Oxford or Cambridge.

All that is known of this writer has to be deduced either from the texts themselves or from the rubrics of manuscripts. In the earliest of his three works, *La Lumere*, or *Luminaire, as Lais* [1]— a Lamp for the Laity—he names himself Peres. Two manuscripts give him a surname. In one, Cambridge University Library Gg. I, 1, he is called Mestre Peres de Pecchame, in an earlier MS., Bodley 399, Mestre Piere de Feccham. According to the colophon already mentioned, he moved from Newstead to Oxford in the year 1267. Next, he translated the *Secre de Secreʒ* ascribed to Aristotle,[2] in which he refers to himself as author of the *Lumere as Lais* :

> Ke Piere ad nun
> K'estreit est de ces de Abernun.   (ll. 2378-9)

(Who is called Peter, who springs from those of Abernon.) This probably means that he was a bastard of the d'Abernon family, though no trace of a dispensation to him on account of his illegitimacy appears in the Papal Calendars. Lastly, he translated for a Canon of Chichester the Latin *Life* of Richard Wych, Bishop of Chichester, which Ralph de Bocking had written for Isabelle, Countess of Arundel, in 1270. The one manuscript of this poem gives his name as Pieres de Fecham.[3]

Everything points to the fact that Peter was a native of

---

[1] [157.]   Unpublished, analysed by Ch. V. Langlois, *La Vie en France au moyen-âge*, iv ; *La Vie spirituelle* (Paris, 1928), pp. 66 ss.

[2] [250.]   Edited by O. A. Beckerlegge (Anglo-Norman Text Society, v (Oxford, 1944)).

[3] [122.]   First part edited by A. T. Baker in *Revue des Langues romanes*, liii (1910), pp. 245 ss.

Surrey. The Norman family of Abernon settled there, and gave their name to the village of Stoke d'Abernon, where the little church is filled with their famous brasses. There is a Peckham in Surrey, but there is also a Fetcham within a few miles of Stoke, and in the thirteenth century two of the parsons of Fetcham were named Peter.[1] In the *Life* of St. Richard the author says that his patron was John of Abernon, presumably the Sir John d'Abernon commemorated by the brass of 1277. He cannot mean " literary patron " on this occasion, for he already had one in the shape of the Chichester Canon, but he may mean that Sir John had presented him to a living, and Fetcham was in his patronage. But with the amount of evidence available at present it is impossible to go further. Pecham may be a mistake for Fecham, but Peter may equally well have been born at Peckham and become parson of Fetcham.

The author has been identified with a well-known lawyer of the period, Master Peter of Peckham, some of whose books ultimately found their way to Merton College. Sir Maurice Powicke is uncertain of this identification.[2] Yet there are certain coincidences to be explained. This Peter was also a bastard, and at his death in 1294 his substantial library was found housed in two religious foundations, both in Surrey, Bermondsey and Southwark. The latter was a house of Black Canons.[3] And it must not be forgotten that Merton's first home had been in Surrey.

The most likely explanation is that there has been confusion of identity here, a confusion which may go back as far as the beginning of the fourteenth century. Our writer was probably called Fetcham, but the existence of a contemporary named Peter of Peckham, to say nothing of the Archbishop John Pecham, and alliteration, would all conspire to facilitate the change of initial.

Peter's career may tentatively be reconstructed thus : a native

[1] Beckerlegge, *op. cit.* p. xiv.
[2] *Mediaeval Books of Merton College, Oxford* (Oxford Historical Society, 1931), p. 116.
[3] R. J. Whitwell, " The Libraries of a Civilian Canonist and of a Common Lawyer ", *Law Quarterly Review*, xxi (1905), p. 393.

of Surrey and an acknowledged offshoot of the d'Abernon family, he entered the Black Canons' Priory at Newstead,[1] possibly after taking his Master's Degree at Oxford. At this stage he began his *Lumere as Lais*, cast in the form of a scholastic catechism, taking as model the *Elucidarius* of Honorius " of Autun ". Finding, as he states in the prologue, which was of course written when the work was complete, that Honorius made mistakes, he began to seek other guides from the end of the First Book. In fact, as a rubric points out, he abandoned the *Elucidarius* plan only at the end of the First Distinction of the Second Book. Henceforth his quotations from the Bible, the Fathers, Cicero, Seneca, Macrobius, Boethius, Cassiodorus and Isidore of Seville are abundant, though he never completely forgets Honorius. But his whole plan, as M. Langlois[2] points out, was much influenced by the *Sentences*. Now if the York colophon refers to the author, the first four Books of the *Lumere* were written at Newstead and the last two at Oxford. If Peter went to Oxford to obtain a Degree in Theology, or even to attend a course of lectures in that subject, he would have chiefly studied the *Sentences* there, and it was perhaps his reading in preparation for this move which induced him to make the modification. The popularity of the *Sentences*, which even threatened to supplant the Bible itself as the basis for theological study during this period, is well known.[3] There was also always at the back of the mediaeval mind the fear of an accusation of heresy. The *Sentences* were " safe ", safer even than Scripture, and this was undoubtedly part of their attraction. Both the fear of heresy and the attraction of the *Sentences* are factors which will recur in the course of this investigation.[4]

[1] But not of course as a lay-brother, as Beckerlegge suggests, *op. cit.* p. xvi, nor as a " moine ", as Langlois says, *op. cit.* p. xiv.

[2] *Op. cit.* pp. 69, 70.

[3] H. Rashdall, *Medieval Universities*, edited by Powicke and Emden (Oxford, 1936), iii. 69 ; H. H. Glunz, *The Vulgate in England* (Cambridge, 1933), p. 275. Cf. V. Doucet, "A New Source of the Summa fratris Alexandri ", *Franciscan Studies*, vi (1946), p. 405.

[4] Cf. G. B. Flahiff, " The Censorship of Books in the Twelfth Century ", *Mediaeval Studies*, iv (1942), pp. 1 ss.

At Oxford, the headquarters of the Augustinians was St. Frideswide's. The Abbot of Oseney apparently had some jurisdiction over the students, who were supposed to be sent from communities all over the country, but St. Frideswide's was their church. Housing was a problem. In the fifteenth century the difficulties were becoming scandalous and St. Mary's College was founded to ease the situation. But Peter would have either to fend for himself or enjoy the hospitality of St. Frideswide's.[1] In any case, he probably had access to the library of the Priory, and on the shelves there he could have found the copy of St. Gregory's *Dialogues* from which he translated, the very copy formerly used by Angier. But it would be absurd to maintain [2] that he was bound to know and make use of that Canon's work, which was then more than sixty years old, seems to have created no stir and was probably long forgotten. Moreover, the Latin of the schools was his preferred language, and his object was to make his known lore available to others. He would, unlike many of his contemporaries, have despised the short cut offered to him by Angier's translation.

The *Lumere* itself won instant popularity. Thirteen manuscripts and fragments of manuscripts survive, and several others are known to have existed.[3] It was never, however, translated into English, perhaps because it was a South-country text. Next came the *Secre de Secrez*, followed by the *Life* of St. Richard, which he can only have been asked to write because he was already famous.

What became of him after that is a mystery, whether he returned to Newstead or had leave of absence, or whether he left the Canons, whether he became a well-known lawyer or retired to a quiet Surrey living.

As a writer, he is intolerable. He was too familiar with Latin to write easily in anything else, he was no poet, and when trans-

---

[1] H. E. Salter, *Chapters of the Augustinian Canons* (Oxford Historical Society, 1922), pp. xxvi, xxvii, xxxvi, xxxvii, 67, 69.　　　　[2] Beckerlegge, *op. cit.* p. xiii.
[3] M. D. Legge, " Pierre de Peckham and his Lumiere as Lais ", *Modern Language Review*, xxiv (1929), pp. 37 ss.

lating preferred to be literal rather than rhythmical. He was, however, deadly earnest and undoubtedly successful in the task which he set himself. He is, of course, out of tune with present ideas of what constitutes literature, and has ceased to be anything but a curiosity. As a " vulgariser " he must be allowed to be interesting, and his portentous solemnity is not without its amusing side. He remains one of the most important exponents of a type of didactic literature once very popular in this country and so has his place in the history of its ideas.

One contemporary must be noticed. There was at Caermarthen a foundation of six Canons which produced a writer in the thirteenth century. A Canon named Simon wrote a poem in three parts [149], of which the subject is in brief " strait is the gate, and narrow is the way. . . ". The first part of the poem consists of twelve tail-rhyme stanzas. The long lines have seven syllables each and the tail lines six. The subject of this part is the narrow way. The next part consists of forty-five stanzas of five lines each, rhyming together. The metre is octosyllabic. The subject here is the broad road. In the last two stanzas the author speaks of himself :

> Frere Simun de Kermerthin
> Profes en l'ordre de Seint Augstin.

(Brother Simon of Caermarthen, professed in the Order of St. Augustine.)

The third part of the poem is an epilogue of fifty-two decasyllabic lines all having the same rhyme. It begins :

> Par la priere de un men compaignon
> Ke mult aime Deu e religion
> De ceste secle ai fait un bref sermon.

(At the prayer of one of my fellows, who loves God and religion much, I have made a short sermon about this world.)

This colleague wished to remain anonymous. He had forsaken the world, and was so humble that he had asked Simon to write him a sermon in verse, although he himself was learned in the

Scriptures and far better qualified to do so. When at home he spent his life in devotion but his profession was preaching outside the Priory. Stengel,[1] who published the poem, thought that the epilogue was a " reimpredicht " in itself, but the sermon or " livre ", as Simon once calls it, is the other two parts of this work, for he remarks that he who wishes to forsake the broad road which leads to shame really has no need of any other lesson than the life and conversation of this colleague.[2]

In the last line the Canon names himself again :

> Et tot cil aient sa seinte beneson
> Ke en memorie aient frere Simon ! _

(And may all those have his holy blessing, that they may have Brother Simon in mind.)

This verse sermon should be compared with Guischard de Beaulieu's more ambitious work on much the same theme. The differences are instructive. The earlier writer points out the wickedness of the world and the necessity for living a good life withdrawn from it, and cites himself as one who has turned away from temptation. He wrote for some great lady patron. Simon was addressing congregations of all and sundry. The emphasis is on penitence, and the poem is obviously part of the wave of enthusiasm for confession and penance set in motion by the Fourth Lateran. Perhaps he himself had never tasted, as Guischard undoubtedly had, the delights of the world. In his own eyes he was the conventional " simple clergeon ", no rival to the Canon who had honoured him with the request for a sermon he was too busy to write himself.

It is apparent that the twelfth- and early thirteenth-century Canons were writing the same kind of literature as monks, and that in the course of the thirteenth century they turned to vulgarising and moralising to a greater extent. With the fourteenth

---

[1] " Handschriftliches aus Oxford ", *Zeitschrift für französische Sprache und Literatur*, xiv (1892), pp. 147 ss.

[2] Stengel also failed to realise that the first section was merely a part of Simon's poem and misread one or two words, including Kernerthin for Kermerthin.

century came a further change. So far, even if the author of the *Romance of Guy of Warwick* is included, all the Canons have a strong religious tendency. The last Canon on the list is a horse of quite another colour.

The much-maligned Peter of Langtoft was a much more interesting and deserving person than has been generally realised. Until recently, all that was known about his career was that he was a Canon of Bridlington Priory, and, since Raine published his *Extracts from Northern Registers* in the Rolls Series, that in 1293 he was absent without leave, falsely pretending that he had the Archbishop's licence to travel. He was then "in Southern parts", perhaps in connection with his writing. But this is far from all.[1] Between the years 1271 and 1286 he continually acted as Prior Geoffrey's attorney, or on behalf of the chapter, either in the neighbourhood or at Westminster and elsewhere.[2] But then the next Prior arose who knew not Joseph, and in 1291 Peter of Langtoft was accused of burning the goods and chattels of Margaret le Clerke. Small wonder, therefore, that he is next heard of two years later "in Southern parts". The explanation of the whole situation is probably to be found in a chapter quarrel, as Geoffrey de Nafferton does not seem to have disappeared from the scene until about 1295.

The fact that Peter of Langtoft had acted as Prior's procurator for some fifteen years argues that he had had some legal training and was probably the House's man-of-business. This is significant, but there is more to come. For some reason the importance of the chronicles of Bridlington at this period has been overlooked. In fact, they had at one point a momentous political effect. For they were selected by Edward I's commissioners as the basis for the historical background of his claim to the overlordship

---

[1] Pp. xxiv, 101. Cf. *The Registers of John le Romeyn* (Surtees Society, cxxiii (ed. W. Brown, 1913), p. 229).

[2] W. T. Lancaster, *Abstracts of the Charters and other Documents contained in the Chartulary of the Priory of Bridlington* (Leeds, 1912), pp. 13, 55, 169, 351, 354, 360, 420 ; cf. J. Parker, *Feet of Fines for the County of York, 1246–72* (1932), p. 178.

of Scotland, which was carefully prepared from evidence drawn from those fountainheads of truth, the monastic chronicles of the whole kingdom. Presumably Bridlington, a Northern House, was gratifyingly anti-Scottish. It is a curious coincidence that Bridlington was to produce, at more or less this moment, one of the most violent Scotophobe historians of all time ; in fact it may be more than a coincidence. The chronicle of Peter of Langtoft has always been misunderstood. People have become exasperated with the early part, which is regarded as too long and as inferior to Wace, and bored by the middle part, which is taken wholesale from well-known sources ; and interest has been concentrated on the last part, the life of Edward I, which is contemporary and authoritative. This is to miss the point of the poem, which was designed as an epic, an epic whose hero was Edward I, just as the hero of Geoffrey of Monmouth's prose epic was Henry I. From time immemorial English historians looked for the coming of a second *Brut*, who would reunite the three parts of the original Britain. In those days few people thought of Trojans as base. Langtoft at one time had hopes of Edward I, but there were to be many further candidates for the reincarnation, including Queen Elizabeth, before the position was finally filled by the unromantic and not altogether deserving James VI and I.[1] There is something tragic in Langtoft's misgivings about the character of Edward II, which he expressed in an epilogue to his work, written after Edward I had died in the midst of a failure caused by what seemed to Langtoft a particularly black piece of treachery. To him the Scots were not only savages of whom he was frankly terrified, but stubborn heretics refusing to recognise the coming of a Messiah.

Langtoft was a North-countryman. He was probably born in the Langtoft in the East Riding, which is only a few miles from Bridlington, where he became a Canon. He wrote in a very old-fashioned style, employing the monorhymed *laisse* in alex-

---

[1] Cf. A. E. Parsons, " The Trojan Legend in England ", *Modern Language Review*, xxiv (1929), pp. 253 ss.

andrines, for all the world as if he was writing a *chanson de geste* in the twelfth century. He uses the same strong caesura as other Anglo-Norman writers, such as Jordan Fantosme and Matthew Paris. As has been pointed out, Matthew Paris seems to have abandoned this way of writing for something more up to date. It is possible that Langtoft's conservatism is due to his Northern origin. That he should have wished to write in French is not surprising. During the reigns of the Edwards York was very much on the map, and there was much coming and going. The Exchequer was at York from 1298 to 1304–5. Moreover, French was still the everyday language of clerics. The *Life* of Edward I is introduced in four of the manuscripts by a prologue which is based on the *Brut* prologue ultimately derived from Geoffrey of Monmouth. According to the version which is probably original, Langtoft declared that the *Life* of King Edward was written at the request of one Schafeld (Sheffield). It is generally agreed that this personage cannot have been well known, and that " uns amis " was later substituted for this reason. It is possible that this Schafeld, obviously a fellow North-countryman, was in the entourage of Anthony Bek, for Bek is prominent in Langtoft's narrative, and on occasions where Bek and the King are at odds, Langtoft takes the Bishop's part. In one case, where Langtoft disagrees with the action taken by the King, Langtoft says :

Antoyne ne fu pas a cel ordeynement (A.D. 1294).

He has throughout the churchman's point of view as well as the North-countryman's. As long as the King is employed in fight-ing the Scots, Langtoft is wholeheartedly in his favour, but directly he lays a finger on the church's wealth, there is outcry, and occasionally Langtoft is torn in twain if taxes are to be used to finance the war. Langtoft's chronicle may never have been circulated in the South. Of the sixteen manuscripts now avail-able, one (Harley 114) comes from the Black Canons' Priory at North Ferriby in Yorkshire, one (Cotton Vitellius A X) from Fountains, one (Fairfax 24) from Bolton Priory, another (Heralds

College Arundel LXI) was written for the vicar of Adlingfleet in
Yorkshire. Laud Misc. 637 once belonged to a person with the
North-country name of Mr. Kirkby, and then passed into the
possession of Richard St. George, Norroy King of Arms, in
the seventeenth century. The provenance of the rest is unknown.
Finally, the last two parts of the chronicle were translated into
English by another Yorkshireman, Robert of Brunne. Thus,
although the chronicle, especially the last part, seems to have been
very popular, it may only have appealed to neighbours of similar
tastes to Langtoft. Obviously, in spite of Robert of Brunne,
French was commonly read in Yorkshire at the beginning of the
fourteenth century. But through Robert of Brunne, Langtoft
ultimately became the source for the English prose *Brut* account
of the reign of Edward I.

Langtoft's source for his first part is probably one of the
Brut chronicles. For the second, he drew on the same sources as
the chronicle submitted to Edward I's commissioners. It cannot
be proved that he consulted them direct. The *Life* of Edward I
is in part derived from contemporary sources, in part from eye-
witnesses' accounts or hearsay. Besides the chronicle, Langtoft
probably wrote the translations of the correspondence of Edward I
and Boniface VIII on the vexed question of the superiority over
Scotland which are in the same metre and style. The question
must be asked whether Langtoft, as well as Procurator, was not
Bridlington's official annalist. He was a very different person
from Matthew Paris, and yet it is possible that the two had in some
respects similar careers.

As for Langtoft's literary merits, they are few, but exist
nevertheless. He writes with the verve and swing which so
offend French ears, but which are characteristic of Anglo-Norman
writers such as himself, Matthew Paris and Jordan Fantosme.
His outlook is interesting, though the first two parts of his long
chronicle are rightly voted tedious. The historical interest of the
third part has never been in question, though the significance of
the changes in the different editions of this section, some written

F

when the English were " on top ", some when the Scots had
turned the tables, the last when the old Edward was dead, has
not hitherto been recognised.   The point does not emerge from
Wright's edition, and the simultaneous publication of all the
" states " of this last part of the chronicle would be of value.   A
study of the modifications and additions made by Langtoft would
be of interest not only for literary and psychological reasons, but
for historical ones also.[1]

Langtoft has always had the credit he deserved for enshrining
in his French a number of fragments of popular and topical songs
in English, not least those terrible exchanges at Berwick, which
caused the infuriated King to destroy for ever that once splendid
port.   They bring to life the words of Roland to Oliver :

> " Or guart chascuns que granz colps i empleit,
> Que malveise cançun de nus chantet ne seit ! " [2]

This is not the first essay in French in the vein of romantic
biography, but Langtoft belongs to a new tradition.   He has less
in common with the French author of the *Life* of William Marshal
than with the Archdeacon of Aberdeen, who sang, a generation
later, of Edward I's chief rival.   Langtoft is inspired by patriotism,
and if this patriotism is mingled with an unpleasant hatred, is
nationalistic and burns with a less pure flame than that of the
freedom-loving Barbour, it is none the less there.   He has an idea
beyond the glorification of a family or of an individual, though
his idea has not the enduring appeal which makes of Barbour a
living writer.

The Augustinian Priory of St. Osyth may have given birth
to the *Life* [137] of the saint of that name.   The late A. T. Baker

---

[1] The present writer had announced such a project before the last war, but it has
naturally been in abeyance.

[2] Ll. 1013-14. Cf. the references to satirical songs in Benoît de Sainte-More, *Chro-
nique des Normands*, ii. 5904 ; Ambroise, *Estoire de la Guerre Sainte*, 10, 653 ss. ; Ordericus
Vitalis, ix, c. 26, cited by T. A. Jenkins, *La Chanson de Roland* (Heath's Modern Language
Series, 1924), pp. 82-3.

(*Modern Language Review*, vi (1910), pp. 476 ss.) refers to the con-
nections between Sts. Osith and Modwenna—the *Lives* of both
are preserved in the Campsey manuscript—but the inspiration in
both cases is probably local. Part of *St. Osith* is twelfth century,
but there are later additions. It may, therefore, be an interesting
example of a composite effort on the part of a Priory.

The list of works which may have been produced under St.
Austin's Rule does not, however, end here. As has been mentioned earlier, there may have been one writer amongst the Austin
Canonesses. This is Marie, who wrote a *Life* of St. Audrey in
octosyllables, a poem devoid of any literary pretensions whatso-
ever, and a clear case of a text written solely for edification. It
survives only in the Campsey collection of saints' *Lives* for meal-
time reading. It is to be expected that this *Life* originated in a
community dedicated to St. Audrey. Only one such is known.
The Canons who had a House in Devon which has given its name
to the place—Canonsleigh—were at least as early as 1285
replaced by Canonesses. The dedication was originally to the
Virgin Mary and St. John the Evangelist, but at the time of
the new foundation the name of St. Etheldreda was added.[1] The
Life may very likely have been written to commemorate this
event, just as the *Life* of St. Giles may have been written by a
Canon to commemorate the removal of the community from
St. Giles's to Barnwell.

Enough has been said to shew that it is a far cry from the
pious saints' *Lives* written by the monastic chronicler, Matthew
Paris, to the political propaganda of Langtoft,[2] who had nothing
of the churchman about him except a keen regard for the shekels
of the First Estate, and who used his talents not for the greater
glory of God but for the advancement of an earthly kingdom.
The difference is partly to be accounted for by the difference in

---

[1] Dugdale, *Monasticon*, vi. 333.

[2] *The Chronicle of Pierre de Langtoft* (R.S. xlvii), ed. Thomas Wright. Cf. M. D.
Legge, " A List of Langtoft MSS., with notes on MS. Laud Misc. 637 ", *Medium Ævum*,
iv (1935), pp. 20 ss.

date. At the beginning of the fourteenth century the monastic Orders had already begun to lose their way, but all through this shorter catalogue of works ascribed to Austin Canons there seems to have been a lack of that guiding principle which is so conspicuous a feature in the case of the Benedictines.

VII

THE FRIARS AND PULPIT LITERATURE

THE two great Orders of Mendicants had in some respects a similar history in England and in France, but while in France the Dominicans were the more important Order, supplying the Royal confessor and so winning the King's support for all their activities, including their great struggle with the University of Paris, in England it was the Franciscans who provided the greater number of scholars and Bishops, and bore the brunt of the quarrel with Oxford. In fact, Canon John Moorman ascribes the failure of the Dominicans in England to two causes : the comparative lack of heretics there and the successful rivalry of the Franciscans.[1]

So it is unlikely that England would produce anything to compare with the *Somme le Roi*, which Lorens, the Dominican confessor of Philippe III, wrote at his request in 1279, and, in fact, there is only one work which can be indubitably assigned to a Dominican writer in this country. This writer is Nicholas Trevet, well known in his day as a theologian and commentator, and lecturer at Oxford. He wrote, apparently, no religious treatise in Anglo-Norman, but composed, in or soon after the year 1313, a French chronicle for the benefit of Mary, daughter of Edward I, who had become a nun at Amesbury, that refuge of so many Royal ladies since the days of Guinevere. This chronicle was later turned into Latin. It is often referred to, as, so far as is

---

[1] J. R. H. Moorman, *Church Life in England in the Thirteenth Century* (Cambridge, 1945), p. 398.

known, it provided Chaucer with the subject of The Man of Law's Tale, *The Tale of Custance*.[1]

Although Trevet is the only English Dominican writer known, it is possible that he was not the only Dominican to write in Anglo-Norman. " Frere Jofroi de Watreford, de l'ordre az freres precheors le mendre ", so described in the prologue to a version of the *Secretum Secretorum*, obviously had some connection with Ireland. Unfortunately, hardly anything is known about him, and his works survive only in one manuscript, and a Continental one at that. Three works may safely be ascribed to him. He seems to have had as collaborator or amanuensis a man named Servais Copale, who was probably responsible for an epilogue to the *Secretum Secretorum*, which runs thus : " Ceus qui cest liure liuront, prient por frere Jofroi de Watreford et por Servais Copale, qui cest trauail empristrent . . . et ausi le liure Dares le Frigien de la guerre de Troi, et ausi le liure de [Eutropius] du regne des Romains. Cest liure est fini." From this it is plain that two of the other texts in this manuscript, *L'Estoire des Troiens* and *L'Estoire des Romains*, are by the same writer. The only other facts known about Jofroi are that he translated the *Secretum* " solonc les exemplaires de Paris " for an unnamed patron, and that he claimed a knowledge of Greek and Arabic.

From this scanty evidence a legend has been built up that he was born at Waterford, travelled as a missionary to the East, lived for a time at Paris and died there about 1300. Now Waterford was one of the few places in Ireland where there was a Dominican Friary. It was founded in 1226. The port is in that part of Ireland which was later to become the Pale, and was always one of the English gateways to Ireland. Even after the original colonisation, any Friars there would almost certainly have come direct from England or belong to a family of settlers. In 1226 some of the Friars may have been of French origin, but

---

[1] [379.]   Miss R. J. Dean, of Mount Holyoke College, Massachusetts, is engaged upon a study of Trevet's work.

it would be rash to assume that the English King would continue to encourage French settlers in Ireland. Anglo-Norman was of course the language of the English settlers, both military and ecclesiastic. It is therefore quite likely that Jofroi was born of English parentage at Waterford, and joined the Friary there. More than a century later, in 1423, another native of Waterford, James Yonge, translated his version of the *Secretum Secretorum* into English, without acknowledgment, so that all trace of him was not lost in that part of Ireland.[1]

Such a man as Jofroi would almost inevitably gravitate to the Schools of Paris, particularly in the thirteenth century, when the Friars were in their heyday and setting all Paris by the ears. He may also have ventured as missionary among the Saracens, but this cannot be proved, and even the " exemplaires de Paris " may be only a conventional appeal to authority. The *Secre de Secrez* was certainly circulating both in Ireland and on the Continent. He may have died at Paris or returned to Water-ford.

The unique manuscript of Jofroi's works (Bibliothèque Nationale, fonds français 7856) bears marks of ownership upon it which prove that it belonged to families connected with Champagne from the fifteenth century until the end of the seventeenth, when it was in Colbert's library. From the extracts printed in the *Histoire littéraire* (xxi. 216-29), it is evident that it is written in a North-Eastern dialect, possibly on the borders of Champagne, and so not very far from its future home. Now Picard copies of Anglo-Norman works are common, and Picard scribes were remarkably successful in obliterating all traces of dialect other than their own. Hence the dialect of this particular manuscript proves nothing about the nationality of the author, and as all the works are in prose nothing can be deduced from rhymes.

A curious fact noted by Victor Le Clerc in the *Histoire*

---

[1] G. H. Orpen, *Song of Dermot and the Earl* (1892), pp. xxv, xxxi. Edited by R. R. Steele, E.E.T.S. (Extra Series, lxxiv, 1898), pp. 121-248.

littéraire is that while Jofroi's version of the *Secretum Secretorum* is intentionally free, and contains avowed interpolations from other sources, the translations of the other two works by him are so faithful that they could be used in making a critical text of the Latin originals. The result is that Jofroi's personality seems as elusive as his history.

There is no reason to suppose that Jofroi de Waterford was responsible for anything beside the three works named by Servais Copale. Mr. Charles Pinckbeck [1] has devoted an article to a collection of prose sermons contained in the manuscript, which he has shewn to be translations of the sermons of Maurice de Sully, belonging to the " Anglo-Norman Family " or " famille B ". These he believes to have been the work of Jofroi de Waterford, on what grounds it is difficult to understand. In a London Ph.D. thesis, written in 1936, to which he refers, he also suggests that *Le petis livres de Moralitez* and a version of *Le Lucidaire* are by Jofroi. His arguments, based on the features of the language of this single manuscript, are not conclusive, and in the extracts which he gives to prove his point it is disconcerting to note that one Western characteristic occurs in the *Sermons*, but in no other text. It is unlikely that Jofroi wrote any of the texts in this manuscript except those expressly mentioned by Servais Copale.

The question of Jofroi's dialect cannot be solved on the evidence at present available. The chances are almost equal that he may or may not have been an Anglo-Norman writer, with the balance slightly in favour of the former alternative.[2]

If the Dominicans are disappointing as a field for investigation, the Franciscans are another story. Their great Oxford patron, Robert Grosseteste, set them the example, but his own writings will be dealt with in another place, among the seculars. Amongst the Franciscans proper are three men who bear famous names.

---

[1] *Romanic Review*, xxxiv (1943), pp. 109 ss.
[2] Monsieur Jacques Monfrin has in preparation an edition of Jofroi's works.

FRANCISCANS

First, the great Franciscan Archbishop of Canterbury, John Pecham. Pecham has long been known as an accomplished letter-writer in Anglo-Norman,[1] but the fact that he also wrote a treatise in that dialect is usually overlooked. This treatise is the *Jerarchie* which he wrote at the request of Eleanor, Queen of Edward I. It was formerly described as a translation of the *Hierarchia Caelestis* of Pseudo-Dionysius the Areopagite, but on investigation it turned out to be a development on a theme borrowed from Pseudo-Dionysius. It is distinguished by an original and personal idea, the illustration of the functions of the different orders of angels by a comparison with the duties incumbent upon court officers. Most of the information about the angels themselves is derived not from " mis sires seynt Denis ", but from the unnamed Peter Lombard, who thus supplied John Pecham, as he also supplied Peter of Peckham, with an un-acknowledged mine of material. The Archbishop also draws upon Thomas Aquinas and possibly upon Isidore of Seville.

It is known from Pecham's letters that he was on intimate terms with the King and Queen, and that he took his duties so seriously that he did not hesitate to rebuke them when he thought occasion required. The *Jerarchie* is a sermon couched in the form of a letter. A rubric in the only surviving manuscript declares that it was written at the Queen's request, and this is supported by internal evidence. The Queen was not interested in the essence of Angels, that subject so beloved of the schoolmen, with its endless possibilities for debate, and upon which Pecham had exercised his brains in his academic days[2]; she wanted to know what they were for, and why the Pseudo-Dionysius had written about them. The Celestial Hierarchy may have been in the air. It had recently been retranslated, with a fresh com-

---

[1] F. J. Tanquerey, *Recueil de lettres anglo-françaises* (Paris, 1916), pp. xiv ss.
[2] Cf. D. E. Sharp, *Franciscan Philosophers at Oxford* (Oxford, 1930), p. 204.

mentary, by Grosseteste. Pecham undertook the work of explanation, and, good schoolman that he was, proceeded to argue from the known to the unknown, and so describes the functions of angels in terms of court officers and servants. This was of course a common trick. Writers accustomed to university teaching naturally employed the same method, one which provides an obvious means of approach, when instructing the laity. Pecham was in the habit of treating the King and Queen like students. Thus when he wrote to the Queen his famous rebuke on the subject of usury, he protested : " E pur ço vus di jeo, ma tres chere dame, devaunt Dieu e devaunz la curt du ciel ". Similarly, in the equally well-known letter of condolence on the death of the King's son Alphonso, " the child who was the hope of us all ", he cannot help beginning : " Sire, par poer de reson ke Dieus vus a donee, vus entendez bien ke nule avantage ne avient en tere ke ne passe avaunt par le juggement del Emperere celestre e de sa curt ".[1] These sentences would be nothing in themselves, but taken in conjunction with the *Jerarchie* shed light on the way the Franciscan Archbishop felt that a sovereign needed his pastoral care as much as the humblest of his subjects, and how his lecturing habits persisted late in life, while his mind remained sufficiently flexible to provide special illustrations to meet the case of Royalty.

The *Jerarchie*,[2] although cast in the form ot a private letter, and framed to meet a special case, was no doubt intended to enjoy the wider circulation which it seems to have obtained, since the sole surviving copy was given to a Franciscan House by one of the Friars there.

Adam of Exeter, sometimes called Adam of Oxford, is another well-known figure of the times who has written in Anglo-

---

[1] Tanquerey, *op. cit.* pp. 37, 48, *Reg. Peckham*, cccclxxxiv, dxc. Cf. for pulpit examples G. R. Owst, *Literature and Pulpit in Medieval England* (Cambridge, 1933), pp. 114 ss. Cf. "A Treatise of 1347–65 ", L. Thorndike, *University Records and Life in the Middle Ages* (New York, 1944), pp. 220, 422.

[2] Edited by M. D. Legge, *Medium Ævum*, xi (1942), pp. 77 ss.

Norman. He was an Oxford master, who became secretary to Adam de Marisco, and turned Franciscan about 1227, afterwards inducing his master to follow his example. According to Eccleston, Adam of Exeter's conversion had a visionary and miraculous side to it. Adam may well have felt a mystic call, but he also had a practical end in view. He had experienced an urge to go out as missionary to the Saracens and the Franciscan organisation and a gray habit were passports to help him to his soul's desire. Even a saint's motives may be mixed, but it is not surprising that his contemporaries preferred to stress the less practical one in this case. The Oxford Friars seem to have protested that a " Professor of the Sacred Page " would be thrown away upon the heathen, and, what is less complimentary to their lecturer, to have feared the effect of oriental wiles upon his orthodoxy. The Chancellor of the university was moved to write them a grave rebuke, and it is curious that the Franciscans, after only seven years' residence in Oxford, should so far have forgotten the ideals of their Founder, then barely five years in his grave, as to have incurred the censure of the very man who had done most to lead them astray.[1]

It cannot be proved that Adam wrote his Anglo-Norman treatise after his conversion. Nevertheless it can be claimed as a Franciscan work. Whether it was written after Adam became a Friar himself, or whether it was written while he was merely meditating the step, and was in close touch with the Oxford Friars, is a point of purely formal interest. The treatise [136] has long been known from a copy in Pembroke College, Cambridge MS. 112, where it is headed: " Le exposiciun meistre Adam de Eccestre sur la Pater nostre ". It was originally addressed to an individual described as " ma chere mere ", but this manuscript belonged to a monastery (Bury or Reading, Dr. James thought), and it is presumably while it was there that some industrious reader erased or crossed out these words, usually substituting for

---

[1] A. G. Little, *The Grey Friars in Oxford* (O.H.S., 1892), pp. 7, 178, 179. *Grosseteste Epistolae* (R.S.), p. 21. Cf. Moorman, *op. cit.* p. 397.

them : " beau sire ". The present writer discovered a second copy, with many variants, in the Bibliothèque Nationale, Paris, fonds français 19,525. It is simply headed " A son treschier frere ", and addressed throughout to " mun chier frere ". The Cambridge manuscript is the older of the two, and the most likely explanation of the discrepancies is that Adam of Exeter wrote a treatise at the request of some nun, which was later altered for use in monasteries, either on the spot or in the copying. Many other unrecognised manuscripts may exist.

The " Exposiciun " follows the usual lines, and expounds the prayer clause by clause. This is the method employed in all such cases, and enables the parish priest or other teacher to convert the treatise into a catechism with very little exertion on his part. Thus a work of this kind can either be used for private meditation, as a framework for parochial instruction or as material for a sermon. The expounding of the Lord's Prayer petition by petition was abandoned in their anxiety for compression by the English Reformers in the Church Catechism, but the more practical composers of the Shorter Catechism have retained it.

The Franciscans in England took on two of the characteristics of the rival Order of Friars. They became scholars and they became preachers. Neither of the works described above are actually sermons, though they are both homiletic in character. Only one Anglo-Norman sermon ascribed to a Franciscan is known, the sermon on the Talents by Thomas of Hales. Unlike John Pecham and Adam of Exeter, Thomas of Hales is a shadowy figure whose chief claim to fame is an English poem. He was probably born at Hailes in Gloucestershire, a place which produced an even more eminent Franciscan in the shape of Alexander of Hales, the " Doctor Irrefragabilis ". Thomas may have been a young relative who followed in the footsteps of his more remarkable namesake. He presumably studied at Oxford before passing on to the Schools of Paris, where he is supposed to have become Doctor of Theology. Certainly his writings seem to have been well known at Paris. They seem to have included a set of *Disputationes Scholasticae*, a *Life* of the Virgin, a *Life* of St. Francis and a *Life* of St. Helena, the mother of Constantine. At the request of some nun Thomas wrote his beautiful mystical poem, " The Love Run ".

The sermon exists only in an English manuscript and was almost certainly preached in England and not in Paris. It is what one would expect from a Friar, a fairly straightforward piece of evangelisation, simple but without any of the vulgarity which occasionally sullies the sermons of Friars. A rather unnecessary allusion to St. Helena provides a piece of internal evidence which confirms the ascription of the rubric. The three main characteristics of this typical thirteenth-century Friar are represented in his three languages—the scholar and theologian in Latin, the poet and mystic in English, and the evangelist and preacher in French.

The only other fact known about Thomas of Hales is that he was a friend of Adam de Marisco. He is thus linked also with Adam of Exeter, and probably knew all his Oxford contemporaries.[1]

It might be argued that all this homiletic literature, though it is impossible to read it without feeling that a living tradition of preaching in Anglo-Norman must lie behind it, was never intended for a public which could be described as " popular ", but that it was intended for royalty, the nobility and the religious only. The same cannot be held of the latest in time of the Franciscan writers. All that is certainly known of Nicole Bozon is that he was a Friar Minor writing early in the fourteenth century. From internal evidence and the dialect of his English quotations it was at first assumed that he was a North-country-man, probably from Yorkshire, but recent opinion leans to the view that he came from somewhere near the march of Derby with Leicestershire, and that he belonged to the vast diocese of

[1] *Monumenta Franciscana* (R.S. iv), i. 395.

Lincoln.[1]   The name Bozon or Boion was not uncommon and was borne by several clerics in different parts of the country. Simon Bozon, for instance, was Prior of Norwich in 1344, and Thomas Bozon held the same office in 1471. Richard " Bozionis " was Prior of Swavesey (Cambridgeshire) in 1343.[2]

Nicole Bozon was probably the most prolific of Anglo-Norman writers, and his output includes many short verse *Lives* of saints, allegories, sermons in verse, prayers, hymns and other religious poems besides the *Metaphors* or *Contes moralisés* [3] which have won him lasting fame.

The *Contes*, in the form in which they survive, consist of a collection of sermons *exempla* accompanied by an outline development. The book is not a treatise—not a *Dormi secure*—and is arranged upon no plan. It is merely a collection of examples tried and found useful, sometimes accompanied by a tale relevant to the subject, and nearly always by a moralisation. It may have been originally compiled for the preacher's own use. It is in fact that form of note-book so dear to the mediaeval heart, a book of precedents.

Bozon as a writer shews considerable versatility. He was not merely a versifier, though he could turn out dull narrative by the yard if necessary, but has even some talent. He used at times the octosyllable, at others a stanza form. His prose is vigorous and straightforward. Present-day readers, once they cease to be first puzzled and then amused by his orthographical peculiarities, will remark with surprise upon the clarity of his style. This appreciation of Bozon's faculty for going straight to the root of the matter perhaps reflects the success of a preacher who must have been popular long ago. For Bozon's *Contes* not only circulated in Anglo-Norman, but received the compliment of being turned into Latin, a sign of their high reputation.

There is no need to dwell here upon the interest of Bozon's

---

[1] Antoine Thomas, *Hist. litt.* xxxvi. 402.
[2] Dugdale, *Monasticon*, iv. 7, *Cal. Pap. Let. 1342–62*, p. 124.
[3] [368.]   L. Toulmin Smith and P. Meyer (S.A.T.F., 1889).

matter and the variety of his sources, which is treated in Paul Meyer's Introduction to the edition of the *Contes* for the Société des anciens textes français and in Antoine Thomas's article in the *Histoire littéraire*. Professor Owst, in spite of his unreasoned prejudice against Anglo-Norman, makes abundant use of Bozon in his two books, *Preaching in Medieval England* (Cambridge, 1926) and *Literature and Pulpit in Medieval England* (Cambridge, 1933), and the *Tales* have even been translated into Modern English, which should ensure them a lasting popularity.[1]

PREACHING

These Franciscan writers in Anglo-Norman raise the whole question of what language was spoken in the English pulpit. Quantities of mediaeval sermons exist in a Latin form, and undoubtedly many of these were delivered in a vernacular and committed to parchment in Latin, exactly as Court pleadings which took place in French were recorded in Latin.[2] Some preaching, however, even to the ignorant, did take place in Latin. This is demonstrated in spectacular fashion by the complacent Giraldus Cambrensis, who records his satisfaction at bringing tears to the eyes of his Welsh congregations, when he preached a crusade in Latin, the only language he could bring himself to use. Latin sermons were usual at the chapters of religious Orders, but it would be idle to pretend that all sermons delivered before an audience of monks, still less one of nuns, were necessarily in Latin. In England, the preacher must often have contented himself with the second best, Anglo-Norman. Thomas of Hales's *Sermon* may easily have been addressed to such a congregation. Friars were exploited as preachers by other Orders, and were regarded as persons specially trained for the job. Yet the difficulty of following a Latin sermon has been much exaggerated in some quarters. Even to this day, every Hilary Term the

---

[1] *Metaphors of Brother Bozon translated* . . ., by J. R. (London, 1913).

[2] A. Lecoy de la Marche, *La Chaire française au moyen-âge* (Paris, 1868), pp. 234, 235. *N.B.*—Entries of Anglo-Norman sermons in Catalogues of MSS. should be treated with reserve. They are often by Maurice de Sully, St. Edmund, Bonaventure, etc.

University of Oxford repairs to St. Mary's to savour a sermon in the tongue in which the formal business of the university is still conducted, and in days gone by all lectures were in Latin. Only gradually would French gain ground. There was probably some difference between the twelfth and thirteenth centuries in this respect.

While not everyone is agreed upon this point of preaching in monasteries, the position is naturally more contested as regards popular audiences. Writers such as F. S. Stevenson, Professor G. R. Owst, Canon John Moorman and even Dr. G. G. Coulton seem inclined to assume too readily that preaching in English was almost universal. Professor Owst even goes so far as to claim that Bozon's sermons may have been preached in English and recorded in French for some special patron. Whether the countless verse-sermons were, in his opinion, subjected to the same treatment he prudently refrains from stating.[1] This question has been approached too much from the point of view of the congregation and far too little from that of the preacher.

Naturally, a congregation of country bumpkins would have been more edified by a sermon in English than by one in Latin or even Anglo-Norman, but the clergy were not always prepared to give them one. Except for some of the country parsons, who were so ill-educated that they knew little or no Latin, and were often insufficiently acquainted with doctrine to preach in any language, the clergy, especially those with university degrees or members of religious Orders, were accustomed to read, write, talk, and in consequence to think, in Latin with Anglo-Norman as a misericorde. Both in monasteries and in colleges English was for long a forbidden tongue. They simply did not possess the requisite English vocabulary for preaching. A writer like Peter of Peckham will even complain of the difficulty of translating from Latin into French. Theology, like the Law centuries later, was " scarce expressible properly in English ". Some scholars have been misled by passages in French quoted in Latin sermons, or

---

[1] *Literature and Pulpit in Medieval England* (Cambridge, 1933), p. xviii.

English proverbs in French ones. The passage from one language to another became a sort of game, and macaronic verses in two or even three languages were in vogue at one period. Bozon quoted English proverbs. Bromyard quoted both French and English in his Latin sermons. The judges of Edward I's reign were in the habit of disconcerting Counsel with salty English sayings delivered with pungent force from the Bench. Langtoft quoted snatches of English popular song in his French chronicle.

Abbot Samson is believed to have been the first person to make a stand against preaching in Latin for " swank ", at the end of the twelfth century. He would like to have insisted upon English, but was obliged to allow French as an alternative. He himself set a good example, but is an illustration of the difficulties in the path of a reformer, since his native Norfolk seems not to have been wholly intelligible to his Suffolk auditors. In Richard Poore's Constitutions, perhaps copied by Archbishop Edmund, lay baptism was allowed in cases of extremity in French, English or Latin, in that order.[1] Grosseteste may possibly have preached in English, but he issued forms and instructions in French. Stevenson says : " Towards the end of his episcopal career he frequently preached in English, but his practice during the earlier portion of his espicopate was to preach in Latin to the clergy, and to instruct them to use the English language in their sermons to their congregations ". Canon Moorman repeats this statement.[2] It is a pure myth. Matthew Paris merely remarks (*Chron. Maj.* v. 256-7): "frequenter quoque sermonem fecit populo ", without specifying any language, and Grosseteste's charge to his clergy is simply (*Epistolae*, p. 155) : " doceant frequenter laicos in idiomate communi ". Stevenson glosses this (p. 133) " that is, the English tongue ", but the " vernacular " was not necessarily English. To Bozon, French

---

[1] *Sarum Charters* (R.S. xcvii), p. 139, cf. Wilkins, *Concilia*, i. 636.
[2] F. S. Stevenson, *Robert Grosseteste* (London, 1899), p. 32 ; Moorman, *op. cit.* pp. 80, 194.

is the "comun langage ".[1] In Grosseteste's *De Confessione et Modo Confitendi Peccata*, which is followed by an *Iniunccio Gallice*, "there are", says Professor Harrison Thomson,[2] "frequent references to the use of the vernacular, but mostly *Gallica* is specified". Obviously, the situation had not changed much since Samson's day. The foreign priest who knew no English was objectionable to everyone, but on political grounds. It is Matthew Paris, the Latin chronicler and French poet, who records with glee the incident when William Longchamp was stoned in 1191, partly for disguising himself as a woman, but still more for pretending not to understand English, and principally simply for the offence of being a foreigner.[3]   The Register of Simon of Ghent provides Canon Moorman with the case of a foreign rector who was only instituted on condition that he had a chaplain to teach him English.   This may have been another pious aspiration.[4]   Grosseteste was actually suspended by the Pope in 1251 for refusing to institute an Italian who knew no English, but this was another political case, and on another occasion Grosseteste declared himself willing to employ foreign friars as itinerant preachers " qui scilicet quamvis nescirent Anglicum, exemplo praedicarent ".[5]

The evidence, as so often in the Middle Ages, is conflicting and all depends upon the interpretation. But only the wilfully blind can deny that some preaching took place in Anglo-Norman, and that, although French was very widely, almost universally, understood in the thirteenth century, owing to the training and the laziness of the clergy some sermons which would have been more usefully delivered in English were given in Anglo-Norman. And Anglo-Norman possessed the immense advantage that it had no dialects.

---

[1] Vising, p. 18.

[2] *The Writings of Robert Grosseteste* (Cambridge, 1940), p. 126.

[3] *Chron. Maj.* (R.S. lvii), ii. 382.

[4] *Op. cit.* p. 92.   Cf. *Registrum Simonis de Gandavo*, edited by C. T. Flower and M. C. B. Dawes (Canterbury and York Society, xli, 1934), ii. 799, 800.

[5] M. Paris, *Chron. Maj.* v. 257.   Stevenson, *op. cit.* p. 306.   *Monumenta Franciscana*, i. 64.

VIII

THE SECULARS—ARCHBISHOPS, BISHOPS, CANONS, CHAPLAINS

A USEFUL standard of comparison for the study of literature produced by members of religious Orders is provided by secular writers. These, like the former, include an Archbishop of Canterbury.

The life of Edmund of Abingdon is too well known to bear repetition,[1] but certain aspects of it must be considered here in relation to his work.

It is often stated that he wrote for the monks at Pontigny, during the three weeks that he spent there, a little treatise which summed up the teaching of his lifetime, the *Speculum Ecclesiae*. There is no evidence that this work is connected with Pontigny, while there is a strong probability that the Anglo-Norman version, usually known as the *Merure de Seinte Eglise*, is older than the Latin. The work exists in many manuscripts, French, Latin and English, and some of these are addressed to a nun or nuns. They may bear the title *Sermon*, or *Some* (*Summa*). If the association of the text with Pontigny has any foundation, it may refer to a Latin version of the *Merure* which itself may have been written in England. There are at least three separate Latin versions ; the translation from the French ascribed by Nicholas Brigham, the sixteenth-century scholar, to William Beufu, a Northampton Carmelite of the fourteenth century, may be one,

---

[1] Cf. the *Lives* by Wilfrid Wallace (London, 1893), Bernard Ward (London, 1903), F. de Paravicini (London, 1898), and A. B. Emden, *An Oxford Hall in Mediaeval Times* (Oxford, 1927).

while the earliest may have been made by St. Edmund himself in France.[1]

The form and contents of the *Merure* [2] cannot be understood without considering some of the circumstances of St. Edmund's life. He came of a deeply religious family. His father retired to the Benedictine monastery of Eynsham, leaving the upbringing of four children to his wife, Mabel. Edmund went to Oxford as a young and day-dreaming boy, and his rather priggish piety made him the subject of picturesque legends there. About 1190 Mabel sent both him and his brother to Paris, and for many years Edmund divided his time between School Street and the rue du Fouarre. He returned to England to take charge of his two sisters, but before 1210 he was renowned at Paris as a lecturer in divinity and as a preacher. Possibly some of his sermons may have been in French. About 1214 he was again lecturing in Oxford, but in 1219 he left the university to become Treasurer of Salisbury, where for the next three years he was the associate of the great Bishop Richard Poore. Next, he travelled the country as a preacher. Finally, in 1233, when staying quietly at his prebend of Calne, he received the news of his elevation to Canterbury. From thenceforward he played an unwilling part in ecclesiastical politics, until, a beaten man, he trod the same road as Stephen Langton and Thomas à Becket and died in exile.

At various times during his life Edmund was in close touch with religious communities. First, when he was a little boy, his father joined the Benedictines at Eynsham. Later, he had the task of entering his sisters at a nunnery, and with characteristic Puritanism searched England until he found one which would accept them without a dowry, the Cistercian House of Catesby in Northamptonshire. For more than a year after he had taken his degree in theology he resided with the Austin Canons at Merton, probably because this period of his career coincided with the Dispersion of 1209–14. During his time at Salisbury he

---

[1] John Bale, *Index Britanniae Scriptoribus*, edited by Poole and Bateson (Oxford, 1902), p. 116.   [2] [156.]   Privately printed by H. W. Robbins, 1923.

was in constant touch with various communities, particularly the Cistercian House at Empress Stanley. Finally came his flight to the Cistercians at Pontigny, where he intended to lay his bones. But this was denied him, and it was amongst the Austin Canons at Soisy, whither he had retired in search of health, that he found peace at last. All his life Edmund seems to have suffered from an inability to make up his mind, and the removal of his mother's forceful personality was perhaps fatal. The time to retire from the world was when the summons came to Canterbury, but just as Roland refused to sound the horn until it was too late, so did Edmund fail to hear the call to religious life until what should have been a summons to duty became a means of escape. He has left behind him, however, two memorials, the Hall at Oxford which stands on the site where he once lived and worked, and the *Speculum* or *Merure*, that redeem a career which ends in disappointment.

There are reasons for thinking that the *Merure* as it stands is a composite work. It opens exactly like a sermon, with the text " Videte Vocationem Vestram ", a sermon addressed to a religious community. It has been assumed, as has already been stated, that this community was Pontigny, but there are obvious objections to this theory. In manuscript the words " vus " and " nus " are sometimes indistinguishable. There is some doubt whether St. Edmund said of his text, " these words are addressed to you ", or " to us, men of religion ".[1] Moreover, it is not certain whether " religion " is to be taken in the technical sense. The religious life, it appears from the introductory part of this " sermon ", is the way of perfection, and the way of perfection is attained by meditation, and meditation leads by contemplation to the knowledge of God. There are three kinds and three degrees of contemplation which lead to this knowledge, and prepare the way for the study of how to live perfectly. Now the perfect life is the ambition of everybody, without as well as within the cloister,

---

[1] Unfortunately there is no critical text of the *Merure*. La Bigne's edition of the Latin is no help—the pronoun is absent.

and St. Edmund's treatise is still in use to help all kinds of people to attain that end, but it is obvious that St. Edmund was thinking only of members of an Order when he wrote, for the people he addressed had unlimited leisure for meditation, except that they had to get up, go to bed, and attend the seven services.

The introduction and conclusion of this work provide the outline of a sermon, but if the development which lies between is read, as it rarely is, with attention paid to its construction and not to its matter, it becomes evident that it may not be part of the original plan. The introduction and conclusion shew two sides of Edmund's personality, the mystic and the schoolman. What he says is pure mysticism, how he says it is scholastic. The part in between consists of two independent sections ; one shews him as a diocesan.

First of all, he says that it is necessary to think of God without ceasing, particularly when rising and lying down. The three kinds of contemplation are in creatures, in Holy Writ and in God. The creatures are dealt with summarily. Holy Writ takes up the lion's share of the treatise. For Holy Writ is contemplated through the means later to become familiar as the " Lay Folk's Catechism ". Without doubt the Fourth Lateran Council in 1215 and the English Bishops' Constitutions which followed it merely codified existing practice, but it is impossible to read Edmund's account of the Seven Deadly Sins, the Seven Beatitudes, the Ten Commandments, the Twelve Articles of the Faith, the Seven Sacraments of the Church, the Seven Gifts of the Holy Ghost, the Seven Works of Mercy, the Four Cardinal Virtues and the Seven Petitions of the Paternoster without recalling not only his lectures on the *Sentences* but also his close association with Richard Poore, whose Constitutions were copied and amplified through the years until the time of John Pecham, who set the seal on Poore's work. This part of the *Merure* is the earliest vernacular attempt to put precept into practice, and is one of the most interesting because it was written before the pattern became stereotyped. These passages are probably not later than 1219.

The contemplation in God is twofold, in His Manhood and in His Godhead, and the way to attain this contemplation is again by meditation, divided, for the convenience of regulars, into seven parts, each preceding a Canonical Hour. Thus every minute of the day will be occupied. Although there is no actual clash with the meditations already prescribed for getting up and going to bed, these are plainly ignored at this point. The meditations before the Hours are again twofold, a meditation on the life of our Lord or " Season " coupled with another on His Passion. This raises an interesting point. There is in existence a copy of a set of meditations for the Hours which has been identified as the meditations on the Passion by St. Edmund,[1] only these are longer than the corresponding ones in the *Merure*. Either, therefore, they have been expanded or, as seems more probable, those in the *Merure* have been condensed. Nothing can be proved on the evidence available, but that evidence does suggest that there were once in existence two sets of meditations by St. Edmund, and that he subsequently condensed and combined them both in the *Merure*. It has previously been suspected that the *Merure* is a composite work.[2]

It cannot be denied that the *Merure* has a thread, but it lacks a plan, and the different sections are disproportionate and unbalanced. This is of course characteristic of mediaeval and renaissance writers. Certainly at one moment the *Merure* was conceived of as a whole, and unless corresponding fragments to all its component parts are found, it is now impossible to disentangle it, but its construction suggests that it was based on at least four previous works—a sermon on the way of perfection addressed to members of a religious Order, a " catechism " inspired by association with Richard Poore, and two sets of meditations before the Hours. The whole work is permeated with the mysticism characteristic of St. Edmund and interspersed with prayers, those perhaps that he had used for years in his private devotions, some of which may date back to his haunting

---

[1] M. D. Legge, " St. Edmund on the ' Hours ' ", *Modern Language Review*, xxix (1934), p. 72.　　　　　　　　[2] Cf. Robbins, *op. cit.* pp. xxii ss.

of St. Peter's-in-the-East. The " sermon " may be one of the later parts to be written, probably between 1222 and 1233 when he was preaching in the diocese of Salisbury, and the composing of the *Merure* itself belongs most likely to the end of that period or to his Archepiscopate.

Matthew Paris says that St. Edmund preached in both Latin and French at Pontigny, but the French text of the *Merure* was in circulation in England, not in France, and most of the MSS., whether in French, Latin or English, contain an English quatrain.[1] It seems, therefore, unlikely that it was delivered first as a sermon at Pontigny. As many of the MSS. are addressed to a nun or nuns, it may have been written for Catesby, where not only his two sisters, to whom he was devoted, but a Norfolk protégée were nuns.[2] In this case the address " dear sister and friend " found in some MSS. may be taken literally. But it is far more likely to be connected with Lacock. St. Edmund knew Ela, Countess of Salisbury, the wife of William Longsword, for whose conversion he was responsible. In 1226 the " Flos Comitum " died, and four years later his widow founded a house of Austin Canonesses at Lacock. It was opened in 1232, and in 1238 the Countess herself took the veil there, becoming Abbess next year. The *Merure* may well have been written for her, either for her new foundation, towards the end of his time at Salisbury, or, which is perhaps less likely, when she herself took the veil when he was Archbishop.

St. Edmund's work was done as a secular, as university lecturer, diocesan official and Archbishop, but all his life he was in close contact with various Orders, and the *Merure* was written not for the laity or for seculars, but for regulars. It must now be seen whether this is true of other secular writers.

The only secular Bishop known to have written in Anglo-Norman is also connected with Oxford, and has sometimes been

---

[1] Cf. *Index of Middle English Verse*, Carleton Brown and R. H. Robbins (New York, 1943), p. 365.   [2] Wallace, *op. cit.* p. 121.

claimed as St. Edmund's pupil. He too had a connection with a religious Order, but this time with one of the newly-founded mendicant Orders.

Robert Grosseteste, first Chancellor of the University of Oxford and first lecturer to the Franciscans in England, is one of the most remarkable figures of the early thirteenth century. He knew, after a fashion, both Greek and Hebrew, and was much attracted to mathematics and to natural science. He feared neither King nor Pope, was a rigorous disciplinarian and treated requests for favour, whether from some great nobleman or from his own brother, with equal firmness and contempt.

Grosseteste, besides being a busy and active churchman, was a voluminous writer, and it seems established that much of his writing, not only pastoral but general, was done while he was Bishop of the largest diocese in England. Before his elevation he had a severe break-down, and all his life he had to fight against ill-health and persistently overworked himself. His output in Anglo-Norman is not great, but shews much variety and completes the picture of the man. It is interesting and symptomatic that he should have found it necessary to write in Anglo-Norman at all. For there can be no doubt that he was a person of humble origin—the Dean and Chapter of Lincoln were later to throw this in his teeth—a countryman of fairly pure Anglo-Saxon descent. English must have been what he had spoken " at home ", yet when he grew up he seems chiefly to have used that language to annoy foreigners. It was not used in his household, witness the grace after meat and the prayer to St. Margaret he wrote for it in Anglo-Norman.[1] As a Bishop, he moved in exalted circles, and between 1240 and 1242 he wrote the treatise on husbandry known as the *Reules Seynt Roberd* for the widowed Countess of Lincoln. According to tradition, his brother was still a husbandman. Grosseteste, the poor country-boy from Stradbrook, become Bishop of the enormous diocese of Lincoln, was well acquainted with his subject both from the point of view

[1] S. H. Thomson, *The Writings of Robert Grosseteste* (Cambridge, 1940), pp. 157, 158.

of the tiller of the soil and the landlord.[1]   But more than this, the *Reules Seynt Roberd* shew Grosseteste's extraordinary versatility and activity.   He was engaged at the same time upon his translation of the Testament of the Twelve Patriarchs, and all the while his dispute with the Dean and Chapter was dragging on in the background.

Today Grosseteste's name is perhaps most often mentioned in histories of literature as the writer of two Anglo-Norman allegories, *le Mariage des neuf filles du Diable* [290]—a verse-sermon—and the more famous *Chasteau d'Amour* [153], which was translated into Middle English and enjoyed a wide influence.

" When men of high estate occupy themselves with poetry, they commonly add little to their glory." So wrote Vising of Grosseteste as author of the *Chasteau d'Amour*.   This hasty judgment springs from a misconception of the purpose of these men of high estate, whether they wrote in verse or prose.   Grosseteste was no poet, and did not pretend to be one.   He merely wished to present an outline of the Christian religion, in particular an account of the Creation, the Fall and the Redemption, in readable form.   The question inevitably arises, when and why was this work written.   The " when " would seem to depend upon the " why ".

Grosseteste does not name himself in the poem, but tradition has always associated it with him, and certain lines of the prologue, which there is no reason to suspect are an interpolation, suggest that this great scholar, who had studied both Greek and Hebrew, did actually write it :

> Tuz avum mestier de aïe,
> Mes trestuz ne poüm mie
> Saver le langage en fin
> D'ebreu, de griu ne de latin,
> Pur loer sun creatur.
> Ke la buche de chantëur
> Ne seit close de Deu loer
> Ne sun seint nun nuncier

F. S. Stevenson, *Robert Grosseteste* (London, 1899), pp. 2, 230-3.

E ke chescun en sun langage
En li conuisse sanz folage,
Son Deu e sa redempcion,
En romanz comenz ma reson
Pur ceus ki ne sevent mie
Ne lettrëure ne clergie.   (ll. 15 ss.) [1]

(We all have need of aid, but assuredly we cannot all know the languages of Hebrew, Greek and Latin, to praise one's creator. So that the mouth of the singer may be unstopped to praise God and proclaim His holy name, and so that each one may know in his own tongue within himself without folly his God and his redemption, I begin my argument in French, for those who have neither letters nor learning.)

Grosseteste was inspired as Angier had been inspired, and he wrote for the same reasons as Henri d'Arci. Neither of them was writing literature in the narrow sense of the term. What Grosseteste was writing was indeed a "romance", but it is presented without an apology, and there is here no comparison with worldly romances. Unlike the Benedictine writers, Grosseteste does not think them worthy of his notice, and his prologue opens merely with expressions of piety :

Ki bien pense bien poet dire ;
Sanz penser ne poez suffire
De nul bien fet comencer ;
Deus nus doint de li penser,
De ki, par ki, en ki sunt
Tuz les biens ki sunt el mund.

(Who thinks well can say well ; you cannot adequately begin any good undertaking without thought ; may God grant us to think of Him, of whom, by whom, in whom are to be found all the good things that are in the world.)   And so on, in feeble echo of Abelard's great doxology.

Professor Thomson would like to date this work between 1215 and 1230, " with the probabilities favouring the early part

---

[1] [153.]   J. Murray, *Le Château d'Amour de R. Grosseteste* (Paris, 1918).

of the period, while the impression of his stay in France and acquaintance with Norman literary forms and traditions were still fresh in his mind. It is furthermore doubtful if his duties at Oxford, which were increasingly heavy during the twenties, would have allowed him much time for the composition of a long vernacular allegory." [1] The first of these arguments has been sufficiently dealt with by Luard as long ago as 1861 : " If he did study at Paris, it is probable enough that he there laid the foundation for his knowledge of Greek and Hebrew. But to say, as has been done, that his object was to perfect himself in the French language, and that to his stay there his French poems the *Chasteau d'Amour* and the *Manuel des Péchés* are due, shews a strange ignorance of what was the court language in England at the time." [2] The answer to the second is supplied by Grosseteste's life and career.

Anglo-Norman dialect is so much a matter of individual taste that to date a text on purely philological grounds is wellnigh impossible. As has been seen in the case of Henri d'Arci, the experts disagree and run the risk of being confounded by external evidence. The external evidence for the dating of the *Chasteau d'Amour* is not apparent and must be sought. Grosseteste had a sister Ivetta who was a member of some religious community for whom a religious treatise in French might have been addressed, but the *Chasteau* is not intended for nuns. It begins like any other romance with the words : " Oez seignurs ". There is a strong feudal and legal flavour about the whole allegory. Man loses the seisin of Paradise and stands his trial. Christ intervenes, and the redemption is described in terms of English law. The Virgin is a castle, Christ the Prince of Peace. Who then were these " seignurs " for whom Grosseteste thought it worth while to summarise his whole theology in such romantic form ?

Like every other magnate, noble or prelate, the Bishop of Lincoln was the head of a household to which boys might be

---

[1] *The Writings of Robert Grosseteste* (Cambridge, 1940), pp. 152-3.
[2] *Epistolae* (R.S. xxv), p. xxxiii.

sent for their education. Two of Simon de Montfort's sons, the elder of whom was about ten, were in Grosseteste's charge while their father was abroad in 1252.[1] It is possible that the allegory was written for these boys, of whom the elder at least was of great promise. There must, however, have been other children in like position, so that this late date is not essential to the theory that the *Chasteau d'Amour* belongs to a group of instructive writings that includes the *Liber Curialis* and *Stans Puer ad Mensam*. It is nevertheless tempting to associate the allegory with the Montfort family, and it is possible that Grosseteste found time to write this compendium of his whole life's beliefs and teaching in his old age. It is true that it is long, but the matter was at his finger-tips, and if that inferior being, Peter of Peckham, could turn out, as apparently he did, 15,000 lines between Easter and Candlemas, that is, in about ten months, Grosseteste need not have taken long to knock off less than two thousand, especially as he seems, in true mediaeval fashion, to have borrowed from other writers.[2]

The language and versification shew little trace of Parisian influence. Like his contemporary, Matthew Paris, Grosseteste made many of his octosyllables too short according to Continental ideas. The editor reckons that 27 per cent of the lines are only seven syllables long, while nine-syllable lines are extremely rare. She adds that some lines can be read " à la façon anglaise ".[3]

The aims of these two secular writers, Edmund Archbishop of Canterbury and Robert Bishop of Lincoln, were therefore different. The former, like most of the monks he resembled, wrote with members of a religious Order in his mind. The latter, like the friars he patronised, wrote for the laity, and like the Franciscan Archbishop John Pecham, expounded a difficult subject in terms of one familiar to his audience, and used for the benefit of the laity the traditional way of lecturing.

---

[1] *Monumenta Franciscana*, i. 110, 163 ; cf. Stevenson, *op. cit.* p. 271.
[2] Cf. Thomson, *op. cit.* pp. 152-3.
[3] J. Murray, *op. cit.* pp. 41 ss.

Besides prelates, there were two other Anglo-Norman writers among cathedral clergy. Hereford was an important centre of learning in the Middle Ages, largely because of its position on the Welsh March. In Wales itself a race of half-Norman, half-Welsh sprang up, which included men of ability such as Giraldus Cambrensis and Walter Map, both intellectual snobs of the first water. One of Giraldus's friends was a Canon of Hereford named Simund de Freine, who wrote two poems in Anglo-Norman, a *Life* of St. George and an imitation of Boethius's *Consolatio*, which he called the *Roman de Philosophie*. Both poems are introduced by an acrostic of the author's name, and are distinguished by the fact that they are deliberately written in lines of seven syllables.[1]

Giraldus himself scorned to write in French, but his friend would turn a Latin epigram or construct an Anglo-Norman acrostic with equal zest.

Simund de Freine is the only secular Canon known as a writer in French. The Cathedral at Winchester was a Benedictine foundation, but diocesan officials were naturally seculars in some cases. In 1158 the Master of the Schools at Winchester was a certain Jordan Fantosme. Nothing is known of his origin, but he had spent some time at St. Amand in Poitou, as pupil of Bishop Gilbert de la Porrée, and had adopted some Poitevin characteristics in consequence. In the past this has sometimes led to the assumption that he was of Continental birth, but no Frenchman could have written his verse-chronicle.

This chronicle [62] is the most valuable historical work in the vernacular produced in the twelfth century. It consists chiefly of an account of the campaign which ended with the capture of William the Lion. Jordan Fantosme is first-hand authority for some of the things he relates, and he painted many vivid pictures, such as his account of Henry's reception of the news of his enemy's capture after he had gone to bed. He was

[1] [16, 55.]   Edited by E. Matzke (S.A.T.F.).

not a good hater like Langtoft, but gives praise impartially where it is due.

In style this chronicle is an imitation of the *chansons de geste*. It is written in fine swinging *laisses*, of the kind used for the description of a later war against the Scots by Peter of Langtoft, but with much less success. His versification has been criticised, but his alexandrines carry the same heavy caesura as those of Matthew Paris in the next century, and if read aloud the lines sound splendid. His style is rhetorical, and the scene when Henry II receives the Bishop of Winchester and asks news of his barons is reminiscent of many dialogues in the *chansons de geste*, and recalls especially the reception of Willame by Guibourc in the *Chançun de Willame* and *Aliscans*.[1]

CHAPLAINS

Amongst these secular writers a little group of some interest is provided by the chaplains. Five of these can almost certainly be identified. Three were private chaplains and two served nunneries.

The earliest of the private chaplains was Sanson de Nantuil, who wrote a glossed version of the *Proverbs of Solomon* [4] for his patroness, the Lady Aaliz de Cundé, who lived at Horncastle in Lincolnshire. This is a work of some merit. Sanson's name suggests that he was of Continental origin, though he himself was probably English born. He wrote about 1140.

A hundred years or so later, Robert of Greatham wrote two works, one for the master and one for the mistress of the house where he was a chaplain. For Alain, the husband, he composed a catechism of the usual sort called *Corset* [249], which is, as he says himself, a *Speculum*. It survives only in fragments. For Aline he wrote a translation of the Gospels, *Les Evangiles des Domees* [71]. Although his sources were irreproachable and he refrained

---

[1] Fantosme is published in the Rolls Series (lxxxii, 1886), and by P. A. Becker, *Zeitschrift für romanische Philologie*, lxiv (1944), pp. 44 ss. Edition in preparation by I. MacDonald.

from presenting that dangerous and pernicious thing, an un-glossed Biblical text, he was evidently afraid of heresy-hunters and stated in the prologue that he would conceal his name until the end. He condemned the envious and the curious, as many a twelfth-century writer had done before him, and at the end let the reader into the secret of his name in order to get the benefit of prayer.

Professor Deanesly suggests that Aline was a member of the Montfort family, since they were connected with Greatham until 1264. Thus the patrons who inspired Robert of Greatham and Grosseteste to write in Anglo-Norman may have been related.[1]

Robert of Greatham's works are interesting as shewing that chaplains as well as friars expounded the faith to the laity after the Council of 1215. In this case a noble family, not a country congregation, was the object of instruction, but Robert un-doubtedly intended his work to enjoy a wider circulation.

The last of this little group of private chaplains is Geoffrey Gaimar, whose patroness was Lady Custance Fitz-Gislebert, presumably the wife of the Lincolnshire Baron who was a bene-factor of Kirkham and Kirkstead. C. Trice Martin, in his edition of Gaimar's chronicle,[2] tentatively suggested the identifi-cation of Geoffrey Gaimar with the " Gaufridus Capellanus " who attested charters to Kirkstead, some of them charters and con-firmations of the Fitz-Gislebert family. Unluckily, these are not dated, but they must be mid-twelfth century. Nothing is more likely than that the chronicler was chaplain in the family for whom he wrote.

Gaimar is much better known and more important than either Sanson de Nantuil or even Robert of Greatham, for he is the author of the earliest extant chronicle in the French language. He had a predecessor in that David who wrote the *Life* of Henry I which he despised, but even if David's poem still survived

---

[1] M. Deanesly, *The Lollard Bible* (Cambridge, 1920), p. 149.
[2] [61.] (R.S. xci), ii, pp. xii, xv.

it would do little to detract from the magnitude of Gaimar's achievement, since it was merely a biography, whereas Gaimar's work is on a bigger scale. His chronicle was a *Brut*, conceived in two parts. The first part has suffered a curious fate, and has disappeared altogether. The taste of the day preferred the royal protégé Wace, and in every surviving manuscript of Gaimar, Wace's *Brut* has been substituted for Gaimar's opening section.

Centuries later Robert Mannyng of Brunne substituted Wace's *Brut* for the first part of Langtoft's chronicle, with the curious result that his English version is in two different metres. The surviving portion of Gaimar's chronicle is known as the *Estorie des Engleis*,[1] because it deals with Saxon and Norman times, ending with a brief sketch of the character of Henry I. It is particularly interesting because it draws not only upon Latin sources, but also upon English ones. Incorporated into it is one of the Anglo-Norman versions of the *Lay of Haveloc*.

The *Estorie des Engleis* is not animated, like Langtoft's chronicle, by having any particular end in view, national or political. Like Wace, and unlike Langtoft, Gaimar wrote in the romantic form, employing the octosyllabic couplet, and, in spite of its early date, his work is sometimes romantic in tone. Langtoft was only interested in events ; Gaimar liked to paint court life, no doubt with his patroness's tastes in mind, and his chronicle should not be forgotten when the courtly spirit in Anglo-Norman literature is considered. Here is probably a case where an important difference between a secular and a regular writer can be described to lay influence, to which a private chaplain would naturally be more susceptible than a monk or Canon. There is not the same urge upon the chaplain " to do the patron good " at all costs.

So much for the private chaplains. The earlier of the nun's chaplains is William Adgar, author of a popular collection of *Legends of St. Mary* [13], the collection which was probably re-

---

[1] [61.]   New edition by A. Bell announced by the Anglo-Norman Text Society.

written later by Everard of Gateley. In an article already quoted
with reference to Guillaume de Berneville, Ezio Levi [1] points
out that the work is addressed to the

> bone gent senee
> Ki en Deu estes esemblee
> Et vus, Dame Mahaut, premers,

(those people, good and wise, who are gathered together in God,
and above all to you, the Lady Maud), and suggests that this
reference is to the daughter of Henry II who became Abbess of
Barking, and died in 1198. Barking was, as we have seen, something of a literary centre which could afford to dispense with
outside help, but the idea is certainly an attractive one, and the
chaplains were not likely to be inferior in literary attainments to
the nuns. Moreover, Adgar must have lived within reach of
London, for he claims that he was translating from a book which
he found in a bookcase at St. Paul's, which was a secular cathedral.
Perhaps he had run " to Londoun, unto Seint Poules, To seken
hym a chaunterie for soules ".

Barking was a famous nunnery, but the greatest and wealthiest
in all England was the Royal Foundation of Shaftesbury. For
this House, it seems clear, a certain William Giffard wrote the
only translation of the glossed Apocalypse in which both
the text and the commentary were versified. From 1292 to 1302
the Abbess of Shaftesbury was Mabel Giffard, sister of Walter,
Archbishop of York, and Godfrey, Bishop of Worcester.
William was probably a relation. The Giffard family was in the
habit of looking after its own interests. What Godfrey owed to
his brother's influence was the subject of adverse comment in an
age when all promotion was by favour. The editor of the text,[2]
the late Sir John Fox, thought that Giffard, like the commentator
he was following, might have been a Dominican, but he is more

---

[1] " Troveri ed Abbazie ", *Archivio storico italiano*, lxxxiii. 68.

[2] [77.] *An Anglo-Norman Rhymed Apocalypse*, edited by Olwen Rhys and Sir John
Fox (Anglo-Norman Text Society, vi, 1946), p. vii.

likely, as chaplain of the Abbey, to have been a secular priest. He may be the object of references in Simon of Ghent's Register, which were overlooked by Sir John Fox. According to these [1] a Master William or Walter Giffard (both names occur—a confusion easily explained by a wrong expansion of the initial W. and the simultaneous existence of several William and Walter Giffards) was Rector of Litton-Cheney, 1298–1302. He had permission to return to Oxford to study for three years at a date very soon after the death of Abbess Mabel. In this entry he is described as " chaplain ". After the lapse of only a year, how-ever, he was nominated penitentiary in the Archdeaconry of Dorset. If this is the Shaftesbury Giffard, it looks as though his connection with the Abbey ended with his kinswoman's life. Now he had not versified the *Apocalypse* merely to amuse the nuns. He thought of it partly as a confessional manual (see especially ll. 644 ss.), and it is significant that in the manuscript, which is not his autograph, but was copied soon after his death, the *Apocalypse* is followed by a verse-treatise on the Seven Deadly Sins, which of course was also a preparation for con-fession. The chaplain, therefore, was a man who might very easily have been selected for the office of penitentiary. This *Apocalypse* comes into the same category as the *Manuel des Pechies*, a work which was popular in monasteries, although it was probably written by a secular for the laity.

The text of the *Apocalypse* is deplorable from the stylistic point of view. No doubt the nuns thought it all the better for being devoid of worldly pretensions, and it is to be hoped that Giffard's halting verse fulfilled its purpose of helping them to commit not only the text but its commentary to memory.

Some other early writers in Anglo-Norman, for instance one of the first, Philippe de Thaun, the romancer Hue de Roteland

---

[1] *Registrum Simonis de Gandavo*, edited by C. T. Flower and M. C. B. Dawes (Canterbury and York Society, xli, 1934), ii, pp. 863, 867. Cf. *English Historical Review* lxii (1947), p. 397.

(Rhuddlan) and possibly Chardry, may have been clerks, but
there is no means at present of determining whether they were
regular or secular. Several of them may have been chaplains or
other household officials.

The parish priest is conspicuous by his absence from this list.
No one who is acquainted with the evidence from which Canon
Moorman drew the material for his book *Church Life in England
in the Thirteenth Century*, will feel any surprise at this. It is,
however, just possible that the William of Waddington who
was a priest in the Archdeaconry of Cleveland in 1275 [1] was
the part-author or reviser of that famous text, the *Manuel des
Pechies*. The point is of small importance, for the tendency
nowadays is to see in William of Waddington, or Widdington,
no more than a scribe. Miss Hope Emily Allen, in her illuminat-
ing article " The *Manuel des Pechieʒ* and the Scholastic Prologue ",[2] advances reasons for thinking that the real author
deliberately withheld his name, and contrasts him with Robert of
Greatham, who, as has been mentioned above, divulged his in
his epilogue. This is an additional reason for thinking that the
Manuel is the work of a secular, inasmuch as regulars, who had
secured some sort of protection by having to seek permission to
write, seem to have been more ready to disclose their names. The
Manuel was most likely written by someone in the entourage of
a Bishop, and perhaps there is some symbolical significance in
the old ascription of the work to Grosseteste. Because it was
translated by Robert of Brunne, who also translated the chronicle
of the Yorkshireman Langtoft, it has been argued that the
Manuel too was written in Yorkshire. But even if Robert of
Brunne was only interested in works written in his neighbourhood, this would not rule out Lincolnshire as the home of the
Manuel, for Robert himself was born in that county. There is
more likelihood of a work of this kind having been written at

---

[1] *Reg.: Walter Giffard* (Surtees Society, cix, 1909), p. 282. Cf. *Letters from Northern
Registers* (R.S. lix), p. 53.   [2] *Romanic Review*, viii (1917), pp. 434-63.

this early date in the Southern Province. It is difficult to assign it to any particular diocese, as all the Bishops' Constitutions bear a close family resemblance to one another, for a very good reason. The matter must rest there for the moment, but the differences in subject and treatment between the *Manuel* and the *Lumere as Lais* and the *Merure de Seinte Eglise*, in particular the striking use of the *exempla* in the *Manuel*, suggests that it was written by a secular for the laity, while of the other works the first was written by a regular for the laity and the second by a secular for regulars.[1]

In any case, whether secular or regular, what matters perhaps more than anything else is that the Anglo-Norman writer upon serious subjects was a scholar.

[1] [158.] The most penetrating work on the *Manuel* remains the two articles by Miss Hope Emily Allen in the *Romanic Review*, viii (1917), and ix (1918). E. J. Arnould has recently published a monumental thesis on the subject (Paris, 1940). For Grosseteste cf. D. W. Robertson, Jr., " The *Manuel des Péchés* and an Episcopal Decree ", *Modern Language Notes*, lx (1945), pp. 439 ss.

IX

ACCESS TO LITERATURE—LIBRARIES
AND MINSTRELS

THIS study would not be complete without some reference to monastic libraries, and that for two reasons. The regular writers aimed at capturing a market, and to do this they imitated the kind of work fashionable among the laity. They must therefore have had a knowledge of those works, and one obvious method of acquiring such knowledge would be through books in their libraries. There may have been some correspondence between the Houses which produced French works and libraries which possessed them. Secondly, if the monastic libraries were in the habit of collecting and preserving works in Anglo-Norman, that in itself would be a contribution to Anglo-Norman literature.

Information about monastic libraries is not easy to acquire, though interest in them is growing.[1] It is not abundant and has been published piecemeal, often in Proceedings of local societies or periodicals devoted to bibliography. Monastic catalogues earlier than the late fourteenth century are uncommon, and the compilers of them seem to have felt rather diffident about books in a vernacular, so that there may have been more than can be traced. Moreover, they had difficulty in fitting them into one of the regular divisions of a library. French books were usually late acquisitions, and were either gifts or the former possessions of a member of the House.[2] Some surviving MSS. are known to have been in monastic libraries, and these are listed in Mr. N. R.

---

[1] Cf. *The Bodleian Library Record*, i. 10. 165 and i. 11. 178 (1940).
[2] Cf. E. M. Thompson, *Carthusian Order in England* (London, 1930), p. 313.

Ker's excellent manual *Medieval Libraries of Great Britain* (London, 1941). Often French works were bound up with Latin ones and thus escaped mention in all but the fullest catalogues. Thus the *Chanson de Roland* itself, which was formerly at Oseney Abbey, masquerades in Mr. Ker's list as a Dialogue of Plato.[1]

The following libraries are known to have contained French books (Bibles, Psalters, hymns, prayers and minor treatises are omitted for the purposes of this list) :

Belvoir (Ben.), Bolton (Aug.), Bordesley (Cist.), Bury (Ben.), Byland (Cist.), Campsey (Aug. nuns), Canterbury (Christchurch and St. Augustine's, both Ben.), Chester (Fran.), Crowland (Ben.), Derby (Ben. nuns), Dover (Ben.), Durham (Ben.), Evesham (Ben.), Flaxley (Cist.), Fountains (Cist.), Glastonbury (Ben.), Hagnaby (Prem.), Heynings (Cist. nuns), Holme Cultram (Cist.), Lanthony (Aug.), Leicester (Aug.), Leominster (Ben.), Norwich (Ben.), Nuneaton (Fontrevault), Oseney (Aug.), Oxford (St. Frideswide's, Aug.), Peterborough (Ben.), Quarr (Cist.), Reading (Ben.), Rochester (Ben.), St. Albans (Ben.), Southampton (Fran.), Southwick (Aug.), Syon (Brig.), Tarrant Keynston (Cist. nuns), Westminster (Ben.), Whalley (Cist.), Witham (Carth.), Worcester (Ben.), York (Austin Friars).

Some of these libraries call for special mention. Bordesley had a loan, which became a bequest in 1315, which is simply staggering. This Cistercian House, where plain living and high thinking should have been the rule, calmly accepted the whole library of Guy Beauchamp, Earl of Warwick, consisting of some forty volumes, nearly all of secular romances.[2]

The two Canterbury Houses and the Priory at Dover owned considerable quantities of French books of various kinds, mostly gifts or bequests. All three have left efficient catalogues behind them.[3] Of the books at St. Augustine's which had belonged to

---

[1] Cf. Ch. Samaran, *La Chanson de Roland* (S.A.T.F., 1933), pp. 3, 41.

[2] E. Edwards, *Memoirs of Libraries* (London, 1859), i. 375.

[3] M. R. James, *Ancient Libraries of Canterbury and Dover* (Cambridge, 1903).

the monk T. Arnold, Dr. James was moved to write : " The secular complexion of this list, and the fondness for light litera-ture which it displays, hardly need to be emphasised " (p. lxxiv). At Leicester several French books, including some romances, were entered in the catalogue under the heading " Decretalia ".[1] Peterborough [2] was among the houses which possessed a con-siderable number of miscellaneous French works. The Evesham books, which include epics and romances, were the bequest of a prior who died in 1392 (Dugdale, ii. 7). One of the most remark-able single volumes is the collection of saints' *Lives*, now in the possession of the Duke of Portland, Welbeck I C I, which was used for meal-time readings at Campsey nunnery.

It will be noticed that in this list the Benedictines are an easy first as usual, followed by the Austin Canons and the Cistercians. Out of the forty-one Houses mentioned, eighteen are Benedictine, including two nunneries, nine are Cistercian, including two nunneries, and seven are Augustinian. Two are Franciscan. The preponderance of Benedictine Houses is to be expected, and corresponds to the studious nature of the Order. The fact that there are so many Cistercian Houses on the list, in spite of the fact that Cistercian writers were so few, does no credit to the learning and seriousness of purpose of that Order, but is to be expected. Their contempt of learning would lead them to prefer books written in the vernacular and, as we have seen, contem-poraries accused them of a love of secular romance. As for the Franciscans, there might possibly have been more of them to record if they had not let their libraries go to rack and ruin long before the Reformation.[3]

It would be impossible to compile a catalogue of all the French works known to have been in monastic libraries. Some-times only one text in a volume is mentioned in the old catalogue, sometimes the title might apply to several different works, often

---

[1] J. Nichols, *History and Antiquities of Leicester*, i, Pt. 2 (1815).
[2] M. R. James, *Bibliographical Society Supplement*, v (1926).
[3] A. G. Little, *Grey Friars in Oxford* (O.H.S., 1892), pp. 61-2.

a description such as " Biblioteca in gallicum magnum volumen " seems to have been considered sufficient. Only in the best Houses were French books properly entered with the *incipit* of the second folio, so that the very manuscript can be easily identified today. Fortunately, a complete list would be irrelevant here.[1] Most libraries had copies of Statutes, many had copies of the Psalter, with or without commentary, and other books of the Bible, sermons, prayers, hymns, treatises of various kinds on various subjects, such as medicine and even chess, useful works like Walter of Henley's *Husbandry* and often chronicles. Most of these are perfectly proper possessions for a monastery. The more frivolous items include *chansons de geste* and romances, and miscellaneous satirical pieces (narrative poems are catalogued at Bordesley, St. Augustine's, Dover, Evesham, Leicester, Peterborough and Witham). Serious works purporting to have been written specially for the laity are not unknown on monastic shelves.

It may be of some interest to record the whereabouts of manuscripts of some of the works which have been mentioned in these pages. The fact that libraries sometimes possessed more than one copy of the same text may be due to two reasons— sometimes they were gifts or legacies from different people and sometimes they formed part of a miscellaneous volume.

Of works by Benedictine writers, Simon of Walsingham's *St. Faith* is in the Campsey collection. Elie de Winchester's *Cato* was at Westminster (now St. John's College, Oxford, 178), and Everard's *Cato* was at Reading (now Lambeth 371). A *Cato* which cannot be identified was also at Dover. Two copies of Beneit's *St. Thomas* were at Dover. Matthew Paris's *St. Alban* was at St. Albans itself (now Trinity College, Dublin, E. 1. 40-177), and his *Edward the Confessor* (now Cambridge University Library Ee. 35. 9) was written there. Bordesley probably possessed a copy. His *St. Edmund* is in the Campsey collection and was probably also at Peterborough. There was a copy of Guischard

---

[1] The writer hopes to go into more detail in a separate article.

de Beaulieu's *Sermon* at Derby (now B.M. Egerton 2710). St. Albans probably had two copies of Thomas of Kent's *Roman de Toute Chevalerie* (now Trinity College, Cambridge, O. 9. 34-7446) (and Paris, B.N., fonds français 24,364), and there is still a copy at Durham. Peterborough owned a *Tristan* which may have been Thomas's. There were copies of John of Canterbury's *Polistorie* at Christchurch, Canterbury (now B.M. Harley 636) and Dover, and of Peter of Ickham's *Genealogy* at Peterborough (now Corpus Christi, Cambridge, 53), at Norwich (now Trinity College, Cambridge, R. 14. 7-883) and probably also at Christchurch, Canterbury. The *Anonimalle Chronicle* naturally comes from St. Mary's, York (now Sir W. Ingilby's MS., Ripley Castle). *St. Brendan* was at Worcester (now B.M. Cotton Vesp. B. 10). Bury owned the *Nativity Play* which was written there. Adam de Ros's *Vision of St. Paul*, possibly a Cistercian work, was at St. Augustine's, Canterbury (now Gonville and Caius 435). The works of the Templar Henri d'Arci were at Leominster (now B.M. Harley 2253), and at Bordesley, and a *Vision of St. Paul*, very likely by Henri d'Arci, was also at the Austin Friary, York.

Of works by Austin Canons, the *Dialogues* and *Life* of St. Gregory by Angier seem to have remained at St. Frideswide's, where they were written, up to the Reformation (they are now Paris, B.N., fonds français 24,766). No less than four copies of *Guy of Warwick* were to be found at St. Augustine's, Canterbury (one of these is now Corpus Christi, Cambridge, 50), and there was one copy at Byland (now York Chapter Library 16. I. 7). Considering its title, the number of copies of Peter of Peckham's *Lumere as Lais* which was to be found in monastic libraries is curious. Christchurch, Canterbury, had two copies, and St. Augustine's, Canterbury, also had two (one is now Brussels, Bibl. Royale 3097-9903), and Joanna de Kyngeston, Prioress of Tarrant Keynston in the fourteenth century, had a copy (now Trinity College, Dublin, B. 5. L.-209). One was at Bordesley. The book catalogued as *Lumen Legum* which was in the Canons'

Library at Leicester may have been this work. This makes a total of at least half a dozen copies. Langtoft's chronicle was at Bolton (now Bodleian Fairfax 24), at Fountains (now B.M. Cotton Vitell. A. 4) and North Ferriby (now B.M. Harley 114). All these are Yorkshire Houses, and Bolton and North Ferriby were Houses of Canons. A copy was at Sempringham. Marie's *St. Audrey* is in the Campsey volume.

Of works by Franciscans, John Pecham's *Jerarchie* was at the Southampton Friary (now Paris, St. Geneviève 2899). Thomas of Hales's *Sermon* was at Westminster (now St. John's, Oxford, 190). Both these were gifts from members of the respective communities. Bozon's *Contes* were at the Chester Friary (now Gray's Inn 12), his *Plainte* was at Whalley (now Trinity College, Cambridge, O. I. 17-1041), his *Proverbs* at Durham (now B.M. Arundel 507). Both known copies of Adam of Exeter's *Exposiciun sur la Pater nostre* were in monastic libraries (they are now Pembroke College, Cambridge, 112 and Paris, B.N., fonds français 19,525).

Of works by seculars, there were copies of St. Edmund's *Merure* at Westminster (now St. John's College, Oxford, 190), at St. Augustine's, Canterbury (two copies), at Dover (three copies), at Peterborough, at Whalley (now Trinity College, Cambridge, O. I. 17-1041) and Lanthony (now Corpus Christi College, Oxford, 36). This makes a total of nine copies. Grosseteste's *Chasteau d'Amour* was at St. Augustine's, Canterbury (now Lambeth 522), and at Nuneaton (now Fitzwilliam Museum McClean 123). Fantosme's chronicle was at Hagnaby (now B.M. Royal 13 A XXI). Gaimar's chronicle was in the same MS., and there is also a copy at Durham (Chapter Library C IV 27). Giffard's *Apocalypse* was at Shaftesbury, for which House it was written (it is now in the Bodleian). Various works of Philippe de Thaun were at Peterborough, Crowland (now B.M. Arundel 230), Durham (now Jesus College, Cambridge, Q.D. 2-44), Holme Cultram (now B.M. Cotton Nero A V) and Heynings (now Lincoln Chapter 199-c. 3. 3.). The *Manuel des Pechies* was at Durham (now B.M.

Harley 4657), Bury (now B.M. Harley 4971), St. Augustine's, Canterbury, and Dover (two copies), at Quarr (now Cambridge University Library Mm. 6. 4), at St. Mary's, York (now Huntington 903), at Sempringham and possibly at Leicester. This makes a total of eight or nine copies.

Out of this list, the record is held by St. Edmund's *Merure*, a work written by a secular for nuns. Next comes the *Manuel*, probably written by another secular, but for the laity, and the *Lumere as Lais*, written by an Austin Canon for the laity. Many of these manuscripts had been the private property of members of the Houses to which they passed. The only two books mentioned as having been in Friaries contain works written by Franciscans. Other Orders were more catholic, but there seems sometimes to have been a local interest in a text. As has already been pointed out, all but one of the manuscripts of Langtoft whose provenance can be traced come from Northern Houses, and there is a suspicion that this chronicle did not attain general circulation except as part of the *Brut* in its English translation. In spite of the facts that the list is incomplete, and that in any case collections of French books were built up in a haphazard way, the preponderance of works written for the edification of nuns or the laity over other works in French is remarkable and significant. Volumes of romances were usually windfalls, like the Bordesley collection, though individual monks, like T. Arnold of St. Augustine's, might own a dozen books which could hardly be considered necessary equipment for a monk. Books deposited for safe-keeping, like those of the lawyer Peter of Peckham mentioned above, may sometimes never have been claimed, and have found a permanent home in the library. The monastic libraries, however, can hardly claim to have been repositories of romance, and to have provided early writers with a knowledge of popular literature. But in the Middle Ages romances were chiefly published by word of mouth, and it is therefore necessary to inquire whether monks had any opportunities of listening to minstrels and *jongleurs*.

MINSTRELS

Naturally the Church frowned upon the trade, but churchmen did not always practise what the Church preached. There is evidence that minstrels and *jongleurs* were entertained in religious Houses. But here again the evidence does not entirely explain how the " cloisterers " came by their knowledge of lay taste, for the bulk of it is not earlier than the mid-thirteenth century, and it appears that the indulgence was growing.[1] The monks had, however, some opportunities of contact with the outside world. The dedication, for instance, or other gaudy of a church or monastery attracted a concourse of laity who were worth encouraging as possible benefactors, and for whose amusement the monasteries catered. The repertoire of the minstrels who assembled on these profitable occasions was not confined to *Lives* of saints turned out for the purpose, though it has already been suggested that these " occasional pieces " do exist. The late twelfth-century *Roman du Mont Saint-Michel* by Guillaume de Saint-Paer, one of the monks, contains an account of the playing and singing of *jongleurs* among the crowds attending the dedication of the church there, and the contemporary *Aye d'Avignon* describes how three thousand knights gathered at the festivities accompanying the restoration of a monastery, and not only listened to songs and stories but watched dancing bears and performing lions.[2] Of all these things the choir-monks were witnesses, near or far, willing or unwilling.

It is possible that a feeling of shame prompted the concealment of a practice which was of longer standing than now appears. Entertaining minstrels within the precincts may, like the eating of meat, have been an indulgence which ultimately won recognition for itself and openly figured in the accounts. Churchmen were censorious, brazen or apologetic about it. Laymen remained censorious.

[1] E. K. Chambers, *Medieval Stage* (Oxford, 1903), i. 39, 56, ii. app. E. Cf. E. Faral, *Les Jongleurs en France au moyen-âge* (Paris, 1910), pp. 29 ss.

[2] Quoted by E. Faral, *op. cit.* app. III, pp. 279, 287.

Some monastic writers, and those some of the best, like Denis Pyramus in England and the prolific Guillaume de Normandie, had been court poets and had acquired their knowledge and technique in the ordinary way.   Others, like Simon of Walsingham, were cloistered from boyhood and could only have had vague reminiscences of what the world enjoyed unless they had some means of refreshing their memories.   Matthew Paris, too, left the world as a boy, but later roamed about it in a way which, however useful, would have scandalised St. Benedict. Yet the cloistered life may have led to a certain conservatism amongst monkish writers.   Matthew Paris himself probably made his *début* with something cast in the form of a *chanson de geste*, and only later adopted the current romantic form.   The Canon Peter of Langtoft was still clinging to the long and flexible epic *laisse* in the fourteenth century.   There is no accounting for individuals, and the reasons which prompted a Beneit of St. Albans to write an imitation English tail-rhyme romance in nearly impeccable French must, for the present at any rate, remain obscure.

X

TWO INFLUENCES—PATRONS AND THE ORDERS

BEFORE the results of this study can be considered and discussed, there is one further point to be taken into account, and that is the question of patronage.

Patronage was as necessary to writers in the Middle Ages as ever before or since. It enabled the professional minstrel to live, and although dwellers in the cloister had a livelihood assured to them, it was patronage which usually provided them with a subject and patronage which gave them the protection which enabled them to escape charges of heresy or vain-glory, and in some cases to give credit to their House. Patronage was a form of necessity which knew no law, and patronage cut across natural barriers and confuses categories.

Before a monk could write at all, the permission of his superiors was theoretically necessary. In some cases this permission seems to have taken the form of a command, and the superiors are in fact patrons. Thus at Bury, Denis Pyramus, when he celebrated the deeds and miracles of the name-saint of the Abbey, claimed the whole body of Seniors as his patrons, while Simon of Walsingham, writing the *Life* of a saint who had to be content with the dedication of a mere chapel, singled out one of them, who was probably his own cousin. It seems possible that these monastic writers were not drawn from the rank and file, but were usually men who held some office in the monastery, such as that of annalist.

The choice of a community on the look-out for a writer was not necessarily limited to their own number. The Cistercian

nuns of Wintney had not even a scribe in the House, and were
obliged to seek the help of their sister House of monks at Waverley. Simon, who came to their rescue, threw in a little verse of
his own for full measure. Edward I's daughter Mary, a nun at
Amesbury, had the famous Dominican Nicholas Trevet at call
when she required a chronicle in French. The nuns at Shaftesbury had their own chaplain and Barking also probably used
theirs, as well as drawing upon their fellow-nuns, when they
needed writers. The secular canons of Chichester, wishing to
commemorate their late Bishop, St. Richard selected for the task
an Austin Canon, Peter of Abernon or Peckham, who was
evidently already famous. Another Aus'in Canon, Peter of
Langtoft, wrote for a certain Schafeld or Sheffield, apparently
someone fairly obscure, since a scribe substituted the words
" uns amis " for the proper name. William, Prior of Kenil-
worth, went so far as to employ a foreigner, Guillaume le Clerc,
to write a *Vie de Tobie*.

Patrons outside the community were, however, usually
persons of rank. Royal patrons were sometimes of continental
birth. The earliest known seems to have been Adeliza of Louvain,
the second queen of Henry Beauclerc. Their court seems to
have foreshadowed that remarkable literary centre, the court of
Henry II and Eleanor of Aquitaine. " Dame Aeliz la reine "
married King Henry in 1121. He died in 1135, and though she
survived until 1151, the reign of her patronage did not greatly
exceed the King's lifetime, since she remarried in 1138. To her
Philippe de Thaun dedicated his *Bestiaire*, the first work of the
kind in French, probably about 1125. Benedeit, who was, as we
have seen, probably a Benedictine monk, had already written
for her his delightful *Life* of St. Brendan. Soon after the King's
death a certain David wrote a *Life* of him at the Queen's request,
which has unfortunately disappeared and is only known to have
existed because Gaimar makes a slighting reference to it, blam-
ing David, rather quaintly, for omitting to record, amongst other
things, the King's *amours*. These three works are different in

character, and of the writers only one is believed to have been a monk. Philippe de Thaun describes himself as the nephew of the chaplain to a royal seneschal, a relationship which he seems to have regarded as his only title to fame, and nothing whatever is known about David.

It is difficult to believe that Eleanor of Aquitaine did nothing to encourage the writing of romance in England. The writers at the court of Henry II did, it is known, include men from all parts of the Angevin Empire, the Jerseyman Wace, for instance, the elusive Marie and Benoît de Sainte-More. Thomas, an Anglo-Norman writer, presumably wrote his *Tristan* for either the King or Queen, but the dedication is lost. Eleanor of Provence, Queen of Henry III, was one of several ladies who patronised Matthew Paris. His *Life* of St. Edward was dedicated to her, probably in 1245. The only work known to have been dedicated to a third Queen Eleanor, Eleanor of Castile, wife of Edward I, is John Pecham's *Jerarchie*. Taste was changing. Prose was taking the place of verse, instruction that of entertainment, even of edifying entertainment.

The nobility usually patronised their own chaplains. The Fitz-Gisleberts had Gaimar as theirs. Here it is interesting to note that Dame Custance had already purchased for one silver mark a copy of David's *Life* of Henry I, when she expressed a wish for a complete chronicle which should terminate with a life of that King, and that she lent to Gaimar books borrowed from Walter Espec. Aliz de Cundé only inspired Sanson de Nantuil to translate the *Proverbs of Solomon*. Robert of Greatham's two works, written for his lord Alain and his lady Aline, are works of edification of some interest and magnitude.

The nobility, however, like the Queens, did occasionally enlist the help of regulars. Guischard de Beaulieu, writing for a certain lady Dionysia, was probably a monk. Matthew Paris evidently became the fashion, and he wrote not only for the King and Queen, but for Isabelle, Countess of Arundel, patroness of one of the cells of St. Albans, and for a Countess of Winchester.

I

Robert Grosseteste wrote his very practical treatise on husbandry for his neighbour, the Countess of Lincoln, and other works, including the allegory *Le Chasteau d'Amour*, for the noble lads who formed part of his household.

Nearly all the works written by regulars were written with the laity in mind, whether they were written for a lay patron or at the command of some superior. As has been pointed out, some of these works found their way on to the shelves of monastic libraries, but the fact that a monk could not or would not read Latin was not officially recognised, though French was the business language of monastic Houses and some sermons addressed to monks were in French, not Latin.[1] There are, however, certain interesting exceptions to this convention that monkish literature was in Latin. Adam de Ros's *Vision of St. Paul* was written for his fellows, but Adam was probably a Cistercian, and a lack of scholarly attainments was not inconsistent with Cistercian ideals. It may well be that he openly proclaimed that he was taking a course which a Benedictine would have scorned. Henri d'Arci was a Templar writing for his brethren. Templars were all gentlemen. These soldier-monks obviously could not be expected to be learned. Some of them, like Henri d'Arci himself, were of course highly educated, and the Order had its quota of officials, trained as lawyers and the like, but it was not of these that he was thinking. He was writing for people whose tastes and requirements did not differ from those of lay gentlemen, only, in their case, there was even more need for a supply of suitably edifying literature.

These two writers are the only two who professedly cater for men of religion, but there were many more who wrote for nuns. As time wore on the amount of Latin a nun was expected to know became sketchier and sketchier. The only collection of saints'

---

[1] H. E. Salter, *Chapters of the Augustinian Canons* (O.H.S., 1922), pp. 14, 17. Sir E. M. Thompson, *Customary of the Benedictine Monasteries of St. Augustine, Canterbury, and St. Peter, Westminster* (Henry Bradshaw Society, 1902, 1904), xxiii. 210, 295, xxviii. 164, 223 ss. W. A. Pantin, *Chapters of the Black Monks* (Camden Society, 3rd series, xlv, 1931, xlvii, 1933), i. 95, 260, ii. 47, 85.

Lives in French which was used for the meal-time readings comes from a nunnery. *Lives* written by nuns do not differ from those written by monks, but the domestic allusions in the second part of the Barking *Life* of St. Edward may possibly have been intended to excite interest at home. Works of edification were written for nuns for all the world as if they were members of the laity. These include St. Edmund's *Merure*, Adam of Exeter's *Exposiciun sur la Pater nostre* and Giffard's *Apocalypse*. The *Merure* and the *Exposiciun* both exist in manuscripts where the address has been deliberately altered from the feminine to the masculine, and the *Merure* was very popular amongst monks, but there is a world of difference between a work written on purpose for monks and one annexed by them for convenience. Particular nuns were sometimes patrons, like the Lady Mary at Amesbury, who patronised Trevet, and the Abbess of Barking for whom Adgar wrote.

Templars and nuns may seem odd stable-companions, but in fact they were distinguished from monks by two main characteristics. They were not expected to be so learned and they were of higher birth.[1] Hence the tendency to treat them like the laity.

Monkish writers, therefore, followed and attempted to influence rather than to form lay taste. M. Faral may ask: "Which came first, *St. Alexis* or the *Roland*?" By the time Anglo-Norman literature was flourishing this question belonged to the past. Verse texts are written in imitation of *chansons de geste* or romances. The prose texts reflect the inquiring turn of mind, the search for information and the love of dialectic characteristic of the later period.

It is now time to answer the questions posed at the outset of this investigation. Over thirty writers believed to have been members of religious Orders have been considered. Of these, a dozen were Benedictine monks, about eight coming from the two Houses of Bury St. Edmunds and St. Albans, two were

[1] E. Power, *Medieval English Nunneries* (Cambridge, 1922), pp. 4 ss., 265 ss.

Benedictine nuns, two Cistercian monks, one was a Templar, six were Austin Canons and one a Canoness, two were Dominicans and five Franciscans.   Obviously, if any general conclusions can be reached, they must be based upon the productions of the Benedictines, the Augustinians and the Franciscans.   The Benedictine monks and nuns wrote thirteen saints' *Lives* and kindred works, of which four were by one single man.   They also wrote three chronicles, two versions of Cato's *Distichs*, a verse-sermon and possibly one romance.   The emphasis is thus on saints' *Lives*.   The Augustinians wrote four or five saints' *Lives*, two chronicles, a verse-sermon, a translation of the *Secretum Secretorum*, a " religious encyclopaedia " and probably a romance. The proportion of saints' *Lives* to miscellaneous, usually learned, works is thus lower than among the Benedictines, and the tendency is to be more didactic.   The Franciscans wrote a prose sermon, two works of exposition and one collection of *exempla*. In addition, the compiler of this collection produced several mystical, devotional and satirical pieces and a series of twelve short saints' *Lives*.   With this interesting exception, the tendency here is towards simple exposition.

It would be easy to say that the Benedictines wrote so many saints' *Lives* because it was their policy, and the Franciscans wrote expositions because it was theirs, but it would not be the whole truth.   The question of chronology is important here. The Benedictines and the Canons began by writing saints' *Lives* and verse-sermons.   The fashion for chronicles and miscellaneous works came later.   The saints chosen were for preference saints associated with the convent, but a vogue like that for " the holy blisful martir " or for " the flour delice of paradys That baire the gloryus grayne ", or the whim of some magnate might at any time interrupt the natural order of things.   The movement which led to the decrees of the Fourth Lateran Council, and the subsequent attempts to put those decrees into effect in the dioceses, changed the nature of all pastoral literature, and gave special point to the work of the Friars, who arrived in this country

hard on the heels of the Bishops returning from the Council.
From time to time men of genius would arise, like Matthew Paris
and Nicole Bozon, or men who were reputed such at the time, like
Peter of Peckham. Their works bear the stamp of originality.

The answers, then, to both questions, whether the fact of
belonging to an Order had any influence on the type of work
written by a member of that Order, and whether the Orders
themselves made a definite contribution to literature, are in the
affirmative. But the answers cannot be unqualified. There are
many other factors to be taken into account. The Orders were a
part of society which has ceased to exist, and they can only be
viewed against the whole background which is formed by the
structure of society. Some secular writers produced works
which differ only slightly from those which originated in the
cloister, and an attempt to define the difference between regulars
and seculars, and between regulars of different Orders, calls for
tact in the interpretation of trivial details.

Some other useful pointers emerge from this study. In
France, there were important writers amongst the Cistercians,
Cluniacs and the Dominicans. The fact that these Orders are so
poorly represented in the list of English writers has little to do
with the Orders themselves, but is almost entirely due to the
different conditions obtaining in the two countries. Secondly,
even within an Order certain Houses are very much more
important than others. Thirdly, geography and its meaning in
history have to be taken into account. Hardly any of the western
Houses are represented, while towards the end of the period the
north-east becomes prominent. Next, the first question the editor
of an anonymous saint's *Life* has to ask himself is, whether the
saint is the patron of a monastery or a chapel, and whether there
is any event in the history of the House which might provoke
the writing of a *Life* in the vernacular. Lastly, it must never
be forgotten that Anglo-Norman was not written by men who
specialised in writing French, but by those who were trained to
write in Latin, and the monastic annalist is the possible author

not only of vernacular chronicles, but of other works.

Indeed, it would be such a mistake not to realise the importance of the Latin background of these writers, that this is perhaps
the principal lesson to be digested. Latin, French and even
English are not alternatives. We know that Matthew Paris,
Adam of Exeter, Robert Grosseteste, John Pecham and Edmund
of Abingdon were really Latin writers, and it is not fair to judge
them as French ones, which would amount to catching them off
guard. We know that Thomas of Hales wrote in Latin, preached
in French and wrote poetry in English, and this descending
hierarchy of languages shews the exact degree of seriousness
accorded to each in contemporary opinion. It is a sobering
thought that the shortest, slightest, most jejune anonymous
treatise, only preserved, perhaps, because it fills in a blank page
or two of parchment, may turn out to be by one of the select
band of Parisian lecturers and scholars. For this state of affairs it
is the lay public which must be blamed, not the author. When
these men wrote in French, they did not write for glory, nor yet
for posterity. They wrote for the ordinary people of their own
day, and did not consider that they lowered themselves or wasted
their talents in the process. Some, indeed, refused to write in
French, like Giraldus Cambrensis, whose friend Walter Map
lamented the fact, for the unworthy reason that he would have
enjoyed a wider public had he so condescended.[1] Those who
chose to serve their generation according to their lights should
not be contemned on that account.

Writing of the late twelfth-century Renaissance, Professor
David Knowles says : " In Bury and St. Albans we trace the
infiltration of the new learning of the schools most clearly ".[2]
Yet these two famous Houses are the very ones which produced
more French works in the late twelfth and early thirteenth
centuries than any others. This may seem odd and paradoxical
at first sight, and yet, given the conditions of the time, it is to

---

[1] *Giraldi Cambrensis Opera* (R.S. xxi), v. 410.
[2] *The Monastic Order in England* (Cambridge, 1940), p. 502.

be expected. And Rashdall came to this conclusion : " The connexion between intellectual and spiritual vitality, in societies if not in individuals, is much closer than is sometimes supposed ".[1]

So the results of this investigation, if not spectacular, bear out what is known of the activities of the regular clergy in the period which runs from the late twelfth to the mid-fourteenth centuries. They may pave the way for future, more startling discoveries, and perhaps some little light is shed by them upon one corner of that darkness which someone has recently mis-named : " la grande clarté du moyen-âge ".

[1] *Medieval Universities*, edited by Powicke and Emden (Oxford, 1936), iii. 191.

XI

CONCLUSION

AMONG the many fallacies in circulation at the present time is a tendency to deny that the Renaissance changed much, or alternatively that it changed things for the better, and to claim that the scholars of the Middle Ages were humanists. The writers, regular and secular, who figure in these pages were none of them that. There is not an " âme pleine " amongst them. That the Middle Ages had something desirable which we have lost, and for which we have not yet found a substitute, is painfully obvious, but no good comes of sitting down upon the ground and lamenting the fact, or of trying to trick the genius back into his bottle.

The Golden Age is a myth, and the Middle Ages have no more claim to the title than any other. The men who lived in them and made them what they were are curiously narrow. Professor Foligno once bluntly stated that they produced no masterpiece in French.[1] In assessing the value of their contribution to civilisation they must be judged by their own standards, not the universal ones to which, since the Revival of Learning, we have become accustomed. The ancient Romans had more in common with their tawdry successors than we care to think, but today you can spend hours in the Forum with only the lizards stirring, and the solitary place will be peopled for you by the magic words : " Ibam forte Via Sacra ". Such an experience is not likely to befall you in the sunny cloisters of a Fountains or a Melrose. No one remembers the Franciscans at Greyfriars. " Heo beoþ iglyden vt of þe reyne So þe scheft is of þe cleo."

Surprise has often been expressed at the poverty of style and

[1] *The Legacy of the Middle Ages*, edited by C. G. Crump and E. F. Jacob (Oxford, 1926), p. 193.

execution of many of these mediaeval works, especially of those by famous men like Grosseteste or Matthew Paris. It is forgotten that ecclesiastics had a reasoned objection to style,[1] especially when they were writing for the unlearned, who could not be discriminating about their purpose and might be led astray. Scholars were indeed interested in rhetoric, and the Englishmen Geoffrey de Vinsauf and John Garland were among the many authors of *Artes Poeticae*.[2] For the more puritanical, Abelard [3] put the matter once and for all : " Plus quippe lectioni quam sermoni deditus, expositionis insisto planitiem, non eloquentiae compositionem : sensum litterae, non ornatum rhetoricae. Ac fortasse pura minus quam ornata locutio quanto planior fuerit, tanto simplicium intelligentiae commodior erit ; et pro qualitate auditorum ipsa inculti sermonis rusticitas quaedam erit ornatus urbanitas, et quoddam condimentum saporis parvularum intelligentia [*sic*] facilis."

The results of these two strains, the scholarly and the clerical, are to be seen in most of the works which have been reviewed. They are too often clumsy and pretentious, or clumsy and bald. Only by accident does a poet rise from the general level. This is not the fault of the writers, it is the fault of the age, and these evidences of a taste so different from our own are worth trying to understand.

Some works would never have been classed as literature by contemporaries. The reader who forgets the immortal lines,

> The gender of a Latin noun
> By meaning, form or use is shown,

or the less well known

> Je suis, I am
> A pot of jam,

the moment the last examination is past may well feel impatient

---

[1] Cf. Rose Graham, *English Ecclesiastical Studies* (London, 1929), p. 181.

[2] E. Faral, *Les Arts poétiques du XIIe et du XIIIe siècle* (Paris, 1924).

[3] *Petri Abaelardi Opera*, edited by Victor Cousin (Paris, 1849), i. 350. Cf. H. J. Chaytor, *From Script to Print* (Cambridge, 1945), pp. 48 ss.

with verse which is only glorified memonics. Didactic verse has
practically ceased to exist, and occasional experiments in that
direction are caviare to the general. What a writer like William
Giffard was trying to do can only be appreciated by those who
are so accustomed to lines like those following that they never
consider whether they are good, bad or merely comic. The
question is quite beside the point.

> And in the heaven he did cause
> an eastern wind to blow ;
> And by his power he let out
> the southern wind to go.
> Then flesh as thick as dust he made
> to rain down them among ;
> And feathered fowls, like as the sand
> which li'th the shore along.
> At his command amidst their camp
> these show'rs of flesh down fell
> All round about their tabernacles
> And tents where they did dwell.
> So they did eat abundantly
> And had of meat their fill ;
> For he did give to them what was
> Their own desire and will.

It is not strictly true that history repeats itself, but it is true that
similar circumstances and needs will produce similar results.

Some religious writers believed in inspiration, but from the
stylistic point of view these writers are often the worst, for they
had a kind of revivalist idea of inspiration, and regarded the poet
not as priest, but as a kind of passive medium. If their " sen "
was divine, it was not for them to clothe it in a palatable form.
Here, as so often, their very humility becomes a sort of arro-
gance.

The standard both of style and language varies considerably.
Guillaume de Berneville, for instance, wrote orthodox French, so
orthodox that he has been accused of being a foreigner. His

contemporary Beneit is remarkable for having combined as good a knowledge of French with the capacity to imitate an English tail-rhyme romance. His work alone is sufficient to give the lie to the table of logical decline of verse in Anglo-Norman given by Mr. F. B. Agard [1] in a recent article. He blandly ignores the factor of English influence, a ticklish matter indeed, but one which is not to be wished away in so light-hearted a fashion. It is perhaps not without significance that the two latest writers, Langtoft and Bozon, come from the northern part of the country. The fourteenth century, the period of the decline of Anglo-Norman, is also the period of its widest diffusion, both socially and geographically. This is the French of the " farthest end " of England. Bozon in particular is interesting for his racy, conversational style, reminiscent of the language of the Year-Books. Both represent the spoken word, but literature in general represented the spoken word to a far greater extent than it does today. [2]

That great scholar, the late Dr. G. G. Coulton, towards the end of a long life, declared that thought in the Middle Ages was confused and, to a certain extent, barren because the writers of the day suffered from two handicaps ; they were obliged to work in Latin and all of them, save Abelard, were doomed to a life of celibacy. [3] If mediaeval scholars suffered through seeing everything through the dark glass of Latin, it might have been expected that English scholars would have suffered doubly through the twofold handicap of Latin and French. As a matter of fact, they did not. French was, even to those to whom it was an adopted tongue, truly a vernacular. When they wrote in Latin, if their Latin was imperfect, their thought was the worse for it. But when they wrote in French, which they acquired until the fourteenth century by " direct method ", if there was a clash between thought and language, it was the language which came

---

[1] *Romanic Review*, xxxiii (1942), pp. 216-35.
[2] Cf. H. J. Chaytor, *From Script to Print* (Cambridge, 1945), pp. 32, 33.
[3] See *Europe's Apprenticeship* and *Studies in Medieval Thought* (both London, 1940).

off second best. But if they thought in Latin with difficulty, they still thought, and it is true that they were so befogged that on certain subjects they were more at home in Latin than in any other language. When Peter of Peckham declared that he was about to translate the *Life* of St. Richard " en franceis au meuz ke jeo say ", he did not mean, as Vising thought, that " he was evidently an Englishman by birth and was not fully master of the French language ",[1] but that he found it difficult to translate from Latin books which seemed to him more natural in that tongue. The two objections to writing in a vernacular—unfamiliarity with it and a feeling that it is an unworthy instrument—are clearly set out in a work by a writer who, though he belonged to a transitional period, led a life which was no different from that of a mediaeval scholar. John of Ireland determined at St. Andrews, where the teaching was in Latin and where Latin conversation was enjoined, in the year 1455, but as the result of a quarrel he left without taking his Master's Degree and migrated to Paris, where he became Bachelor in 1459 and Licentiate next year. He did not return to Scotland to live until 1483. In the *Meroure of Wyssdome*, which he wrote in 1490, he explains that he wrote it " in the commoune langage of þis cuntre. Bot in the tovnge þat j know bettir, þat js, latin, j maid to þi fadere in gud mynd thre bukis . . . in Pariss etc." He adds : " J knaw þat Gowere, chauceire, the monk of berry and mony wthire has writtin jn ynglis tonge richt wisly, induceand personis to lefe vicis and folow wertuis ".[2] In earlier days there had been no need to be so explicit. Everyone knew these things and did not question them. The second objection does not arise in the present context, for the writers were in favour of using the vernacular for edification, but they were fighting a battle, not celebrating a victory.

The second of Dr. Coulton's handicaps bore more hardly on

[1] *Anglo-Norman Language and Literature* (London, 1923), p. 17.

[2] Johannes de Irlandia, *The Meroure of Wyssdome*, edited by Charles Macpherson (S.T.S., N.S. xix, 1926), p. 164, cited by W. Mackay Mackenzie, *The Poems of William Dunbar* (Edinburgh, 1932), p. xii.

the regular than on the secular writers. The Papal registers bear witness to the number of priests' sons who followed in their fathers' steps and required a dispensation to do so. The old tradition of the married priest died hard in England, harder still in Wales—where in the diocese of St. Asaph, in 1222, it is said that " bastards of priests and parsons succeed, as of right, to their father's churches, and that the said Bishop takes money from many such bastards when a church becomes void ".¹ The thing, however, was common in Europe,² and it was not wholly bad, even though few can have had the companionship of an Héloïse. The *liaison* which produced Herbert Poore, Bishop of Salisbury, and his more famous brother Richard, successively Bishop of Chichester, Salisbury and Durham, the sons of Richard of Ilchester, Bishop of Winchester, could hardly have been a casual one. For the regulars there was no way out, and if they sinned they did so without any of the compensations which the secular clergy could derive from their lapses. But exceptions do but prove the rule ; intellectual society was intended to be celibate and therefore artificial—Rabelais suffered from it and attacked it in his visionary Abbaye de Theleme and the Reformers sang a " very sensible ballad " on the subject :

> " God send euerie Preist ane wyfe,
> And euerie Nunne ane man,
> That thay mycht leue that haly lyfe,
> As first the Kirk began." ³

The disadvantage, however, was not entirely removed by the Reformation, and it is only within living memory that Oxford and Cambridge recognised the fact that life in a villa, with a nursery, garage and kitchen sink, may be the lesser of two evils for the scholar.

Life in the cloister was not itself a source of poetic inspiration.

¹ *Cal. Pap. Let.* i. 85.
² Cf. the interesting discussion of the point by J. Lesellier, " Deux Enfants naturels de Rabelais légitimés par le pape Paul III ", *Humanisme et Renaissance*, v (1938), pp. 547-70.
³ *The Gude and Godlie Ballatis*, ed. A. F. Mitchell (S.T.S. xxxix, 1897), p. 188.

The kind of spirit which frets not at the convent's narrow room is unlikely to have been creative. The sterner type of writer like Guischard de Beaulieu rejoices only in the asceticism of his existence. If a writer wished to glorify his House, he did so by praising its patron saint. If Matthew Paris, in his *Life* of St. Edward, eulogises the buildings of Westminster Abbey, so that it was pardonable to assume that the work was written by a Westmonasterian, he does so for the same reason that the unknown author of *Pelerinage de Charlemagne* describes the exotic splendours of the palace at Constantinople. The only emotion it is possible to detect is a desire to play to the gallery, mixed with a little worldly pride. And all this, restrictive as it is, was perfectly natural, as may be seen by what happened next.

> If thou would'st view fair Melrose aright,
> Go visit it by the pale moonlight.

Many people today would regard the famous passage beginning with these lines as the purest nineteenth-century romanticism. They would be quite wrong. No sooner was the Dissolution an accomplished fact than the monasteries were enveloped in a mist of sentiment. Rarely did even the Wizard of the North succeed in evoking an atmosphere as true to life as the mixture of bewilderment, passion and melancholy which forms the background to *The Abbot*. The business-like and matter-of-fact tone of the Customaries and Observances gives way almost at once to the intolerable nostalgia of the *Rites of Durham*,[1] with their lament over the passing of the aired face-towels. Thomas Elfrede, a Westminster monk, settled down happily as a prebendary of the new Collegiate Foundation, ending up as vice-dean. But when he died, they found that he desired to be buried against the South Door, in what was " sometyme the processione way ".[2] A ballad writer in Elizabeth's reign could personify

---

[1] Surtees Society, cvii (1902), p. 79.
[2] E. H. Pearce, *Monks of Westminster* (Cambridge, 1916), pp. x, 176.

Walsingham, and endow the building with spurious glories.

> Levell, levell with the ground
> The Towres doe lye,
> Which with their golden glitt'ring tops
> Pearsed oute to the skeye.[1]

The matter can be pushed further back still. All that was necessary in order to be emotional about a monastery was not to be a dweller within its walls.

> Allone as I went up and doun
> In ane Abbay was fair to se,
> Thinkand quhat consolatioun
> Was best in to adversitie,
> On caiss I kest on syd myne E,
> And saw this writtin upoun a wall :
> " Off quhat estait, man, that thow be,
> Obey and thank thy God of all ".[2]

The adage was the theme of an earlier poem in the later Middle Ages, but only this one of them is in immortal verse.[3] Today the words inevitably conjure up the stately fane of Dunfermline, even to the damp smell of the walls and the rushing of the water down below. Place and poem are indissolubly mingled in the imagination, but the man who bequeathed this pleasure to later ages was not a monk, but the Master of the Abbey School.

Indeed, when all the differences which mark off those who inhabit the world today from those who withdrew from it during the Middle Ages are considered, the wonder is that they produced anything which is intelligible. Yet it is easy to exaggerate. The present is heir to the past. If you stand at the East End of the noblest of Augustinian cathedrals, you see nothing but the turf and the stones, hear nothing but the wind and the sea and the rooks and the gulls. Westward there springs a tower, mediaeval

---

[1] " A Lament for Walsingham ", quoted by the Rev. J. C. Cox, *V.C.H. Norfolk*, ii. 401.

[2] Robert Henryson, *Poems*, ed. H. Harvey Wood (Edinburgh, 1933), p. 195.

[3] Contrast the lame opening : " Bi a wey wandryng as I went Sore I syked for serwyng sad ", *Minor Poems of the Vernon MS.* (E.E.T.S. cvii, 1901), ii. 688.

indeed, but which looked when it was new on a martyr's burning. Under it the young men pass in and out—yesterday in Air Force Blue or scarlet gown. Centuries divide St. Rule's from St. Salvator's, but one street links them both, and it is in the company of George Buchanan that you pass from the shadows into the light.

APPENDIX

ANGLO-NORMAN VERSIFICATION

REFERENCE has frequently been made in these pages to the peculiarities of Anglo-Norman versification. This is a highly controversial subject, but for the benefit of those to whom it is unfamiliar, a few brief remarks upon the question are here appended.

It is a fact beyond dispute that little Anglo-Norman verse exists which scans in a way which would pass muster in France. The French system of versification, whose foundation is the strict counting of syllables and where stress is of minor importance, is obviously not applied in the great majority of cases. What is controversial is the explanation of this state of affairs. Roughly speaking, those who in the past have pronounced upon the subject are divided into two camps : those (mostly French) who hold that writers in Anglo-Norman could not and would not count their syllables, and possessed no ear for verse, and those (mostly German) who take the more charitable view that their verse is not based upon the syllable-count, but upon stress-accent, as in English.

The best and fairest summary of the controversy is that of the late Johann Vising, *Anglo-Norman Language and Literature* (London, 1923), pp. 79 ss., but Vising was one of the leaders of the " French " school of thought, and he follows his summary by a statement of his own views, some of which will not stand up to the weight of evidence accumulated in the present study. More recently, unbiased studies of Anglo-Norman versification have appeared in the Introductions to the late E. G. R. Waters's edition of *The Anglo-Norman Voyage of St. Brendan* by Benedeit (Oxford, 1928) and the editions published by the Anglo-Norman Text Society, especially Professor Pope's *La Seinte Resureccion* (Oxford, 1943) and Mr. O. A. Beckerlegge's *Le Secre de Secrez* (Oxford, 1944).

Most writers on this subject have started with the assumption that Old French versification was practically identical with Modern, and that there was an absolute standard of perfection which was invariably applied. This assumption is quite unwarranted. Crestien de Troyes wrote verse of monotonous regularity, but other writers used greater freedom. There never has been a comprehensive study of the field. We are chiefly dependent for our knowledge of it upon introductions to various editions. Formerly, editors were as unscrupulous in emending "faulty" versification as they were in emending "faulty" grammar. It is probable that the gap between Anglo-Norman and Continental versification is less than has been supposed, just as the gap in grammatical accuracy is undoubtedly narrower.

The fact remains, however, that in the mouths of speakers, whatever their origin, born or bred on English soil, French was from the first pronounced with the heavy expiratory accent characteristic of the English language. This is shewn not only by the instability of the "feminine *e*" in Anglo-Norman, but by the change, loss or addition of prefixes. The result is that it is just as difficult to write syllabic verse in Anglo-Norman as it is in English, and the French rules of hiatus and elision are impossible to apply. It is possible to imagine that a system of Anglo-Norman versification based on stress could have been evolved without any direct influence of English. That stress came to be regarded as the equivalent of length is suggested by the fact, frequently alluded to above, that while a seven-syllable line is common in "octosyllabic" verse, longer lines are comparatively rare. In some cases a deliberate modification of the French habits may be observed. Sometimes the "feminine *e*" of the rhyme-word counts as the eighth syllable, whereas in Continental verse it is an extra (except in the case of Guillaume de Deguilleville). This kind of line is regularly used by one of the earliest and most correct from the point of view of language of the Anglo-Norman writers, and one who attains a high degree of literary merit, Benedeit, author of the *Life* of St. Brendan. The slight caesura which seems to have divided the octosyllable survived later in Anglo-Norman than on the Continent and the caesura in longer lines sometimes fell after a "feminine *e*" after the sixth syllable. This was called by Vising the "Anglo-Norman caesura".

In these three ways Anglo-Norman writers diverged from the current French practice, but nevertheless the system itself is unchanged and is based upon the counting of syllables. The most that can be said is that the modifications may have been due to the heavier speech-stress. It is possible, too, that inadequate attention has been paid to the influence of Late Latin verse as written in England. It is, however, idle to deny that in some cases English influence may be detected. Apart from the innumerable instances where the beat can be heard if the verse is read aloud, there is the trump card, which does not seem to have been played before, of Beneit's *Life* of St. Thomas, which is an imitation of an English tail-rhyme romance as far as the versification is concerned.

Scribes often played havoc with the author's intentions. This is disputed by Vising (p. 83), but is proved in cases where it is possible to compare earlier and later MSS. of the same text. Cf. Professor Pope's introduction to the Resurrection play cited above and Mr. F. B. Agard's article on Thomas of Kent in the *Romanic Review*, xxiii (1942), pp. 216-55, where, however, he has confused scribal practice with versification. Anglo-Norman scribes omitted or added " feminine *e*'s " or other weak syllables, and substituted shorter or longer forms of a word as fancy dictated. By drastic emendation it is often possible to rewrite Anglo-Norman verse on Continental lines by reversing the process, or rather by imitating it, but this is to be condemned along with all other hypothetical reconstructions of texts.

As regards rhyme, Anglo-Norman writers were generally careful and employed rich rhymes, though naturally rhymes which are dialectically correct but bad from the French point of view are common, and there are instances of poor rhyming. It is not unusual to find the same rhyme repeated several times, not only an even, but an odd number of times, so that the " couplet " may be stretched to three, four or five lines. This has been stated to be peculiar to Anglo-Norman, but this is an exaggeration. The early thirteenth-century writer of romances, Jehan Renart, for instance, who was an unconventional composer of verse, even employing the rare device of rhyming masculine and feminine endings together, often uses the same rhyme four times running, and in one case probably three times (*Le Lai de l'Ombre*, edited by J. Orr (Edinburgh, 1948), p. 32). The slightly later anonymous author of the *Roman du comte de Poitiers* (edited by B. Malmberg, Lund and Copenhagen, 1940) also employs series of four rhymes and one—ll. 1201-3—of three. In Anglo-Norman this repetition may be an earlier development ; series of four rhymes occur, for instance, in the twelfth-century *Jeu d'Adam*, a remarkably fine work from every point of view, but it is to be noted that the Norman Wace, also a twelfth-century writer, was fond of rhymes in fours.

Vising makes the astounding statement (*op. cit.* p. 81) : " The Anglo-Norman poets were in general, even if they belonged to the clergy, people of little learning and what they possessed least of all was system and theory. Most of them did not know English or knew it only imperfectly, and at the same time they found no little difficulty, as they themselves admit, in handling the French language and French versification. How was it possible for them to construct out of two metrical systems they hardly knew a new and very complicated system ? "

To answer these points *seriatim* :

(1) The clergy of little learning include Matthew Paris, Robert Grosseteste and Jordan Fantosme, all of whom come under fire from Vising for writing incorrect verse.

(2) The complete bilingualism of the country from an early date, being something quite outside modern experience, has not been grasped by Vising.

(3) The admissions of difficulty in handling the French language and versification were conventional apologies, sometimes a form of mock humility, and should be discounted.

(4) It is not necessary to study a system of versification in order to write verse. Anyone who had ever been rocked in an English cradle would know enough about English rhythm.

Vising also says (*op. cit.* p. 79) that " a poet was often satisfied if he wrote lines of approximatively the same length. The earliest writer to exhibit features of this kind is Jourdain Fantosme." Fantosme had been a pupil of Gilbert de la Porrée in Poitiers, and had become Master of the Schools in the diocese of Winchester. It would be odd if his only idea of versification was that lines should be of approximately the same length. What most writers on this subject fail to realise, even if they pay lip-service to it, is that the poets wrote to satisfy not the eye, but the ear. Fantosme's lines were written to be recited, perhaps chanted, aloud. They scan perfectly well when read aloud, and go with a magnificent swing. This is not true of all Anglo-Norman verse. William Giffard was a learned man, but he wrote, and perhaps intended to write, pùre doggerel. The versification of translators sometimes suffers from a desire to be literal. Mr. Becker-legge points out in his edition of Peter of Peckham (or Abernon) cited above that the personal parts of the poem run more smoothly than the actual translation of the *Secre de Secreẓ*. Metres, also, may be mixed.

The present writer agrees with Paul Meyer's dictum : " Il n'existe pas, selon moi, de règle générale s'appliquant à la versification des poètes français d'Angleterre " (*Vie de S. Thomas de Cantorbéry*

(S.A.T.F., 1885), p. xxxi). But this is not incompatible with the " German " theory. Anglo-Norman versification, like the dialect itself, probably varied from individual to individual, even from time to time in the life of an individual, according to opportunities of contact with France, and presents the same mixture of archaisms and innovations. The English stress-system was often combined with the French syllable - system with results of varying success, partly through English influence, more perhaps because of the nature of the dialect itself. The compromise which has produced our modern English system of versification was being hammered out simultaneously in Anglo-Norman and in the English language. In versification, as in expression generally, the learned were hampered by their training in, and familiarity with, the Latin of the schools.

INDEX

Abelard, Peter 99, 129, 131
Abernon, Family of 64-6
  John of, Kt. 65
  Peter of, *see* Peckham
Adam, Jeu d' 62, 139
Adeliza of Louvain, Queen 47, 120
Adgar, William 13, 17, 105, 106, 123
Adlingfleet (Yorks), Vicar of 73
Ælfric 34
Ailred of Rievaulx 24
Alban, St., Protomartyr 19
  Life of 21-4, 26-9, 61, 113
Alexander, Latin compilation 38, 40. *See also Roman de Toute Chevalerie*
Alexis, St., *Life* of 34, 35, 123
Aliscans 103
Amesbury (Wilts), Benedictine Abbey 77, 120, 123
Ancrene Riwle 48
Angier of St. Frideswide's 6, 61-3, 67, 99, 114
Anjou 61
Anonimalle Chronicle 45, 114
Antichrist 56
Apocalypse 106, 107, 115, 123
Arnold, T., of St. Augustine's 112, 116
Arundel, Isabelle Countess of 26, 27, 64, 121
Audrey, St., *Life* of 50, 75, 115
Augustine, St., Archbishop of Canterbury 61
Augustinian Order 4, 15, 16, 51, 57-76, 112, 114-16, 124
Aye d'Avignon 117

Barbour, John, Archdeacon of Aberdeen 74
Barking (Essex), Benedictine Abbey 49-51, 106, 120, 123
Barnwell (Cambs), Augustinian Priory 58-61, 75
  Hermitage of St. Andrew 58-60
Beaulieu (Beds), Benedictine Priory 31-5
  (Hants), Cistercian Abbey 32
Bede, the Venerable 4, 50
Bedford, William of, Prior of Barnwell 59
Bek, Anthony, Bishop of Durham 72
Belvoir (Lincs), Benedictine Priory 111
Benedeit, author of *St. Brendan* 46, 47, 49, 56, 120, 137, 138
Benedictine Order, 3-52, 54, 57, 62, 76, 99, 112-14, 122-4

Beneit, of St. Albans 19, 20, 31, 47, 113, 118, 131, 139
Benjamin, " Danz " 10
Benoît de Sainte-More 121
Bermondsey (Surrey), Benedictine Abbey 65
Bestiaire 120
Beufu, William 91
Bible, Holy 66
Bocking, Ralph de 64
Boethius 66
Bolton (Yorks), Augustinian Priory 72, 111, 115
Boniface VIII, Pope 73
Bordesley (Worcs), Cistercian Abbey 111, 113, 114, 116
Bozon, Nicole 85-9, 115, 125, 131
  Richard, Prior of Swavesey 86
  Simon, Prior of Norwich 86
  Thomas, Prior of Norwich 86
Brendan, St., *Life* of 30, 46, 47, 49, 51, 58, 114, 120, 137, 138
Bridlington (Yorks), Augustinian Priory 70-4
Bromyard, John 89
Brunne, Robert Mannyng of 73, 105, 108
Brut chronicles 45, 46, 72, 73, 105, 116
Bunyan, John 52
Burton (Derby), Benedictine Abbey 44
Bury St. Edmunds (Suffolk), Benedictine Abbey 4, 6-20, 44, 48, 83, 111, 114, 116, 119, 123, 126
  Chapel of St. Faith 10
  Church of St. Mary 10
Byland (Yorks), Cistercian Abbey 111, 114

Caermarthen (S. Wales) 68, 69
Calne, Salisbury, Prebend of 92
Cambridge 57-61, 64
  Church of St. Giles 57, 75
Campsey (Suffolk), Augustinian Priory 75, 111-13, 115, 123
Canonsleigh (Devon), Augustinian Priory 75
Canterbury (Kent) 45
  Christchurch, Benedictine Cathedral Priory 45, 111, 114
  St. Augustine's, Benedictine Abbey 45, 111, 113-16
  See of 92, 93
Canterbury, John of 45, 114